LAKELAND
VILLAGES

"In choosing the Lake District for his studies, the pen and ink artist is immediately at the disadvantage of having to register in black and white the most colourful region in the country."

A. Wainwright.

Blencathra and the Glenderamackin Valley

LAKELAND VILLAGES

Jim Watson

CICERONE PRESS · MILNTHORPE · CUMBRIA

First published 1988
Reprinted 1990

ISBN 1 85284 024 2

For
Maureen
Tim and Holly

'Home is where the heart is'

Askham.

Dacre.

Introduction

I grew up in two Lakeland villages. Only now, after living in a town for nearly thirty years do I realise how privileged I was. To live in a small, safe community, with plenty to do amongst stunning scenery is something too many modern youngsters miss.

This book was my chance to return to familiar stamping grounds, explore others that I partly knew, and seek out some new places that were only names on the map. What a prospect! What a delight!

There is no typical Lakeland village. Their sizes, looks and characters are as varied as the Lake District landscape. Some are hardly villages at all. Others are small towns.

Many were originally mining or quarrying communities or involved in the extensive Cumbrian woollen industry. Some were part of the forestry plantations or groups of workers' houses for numerous factories turning out wooden products. Scattered farmsteads have populated the remote dales for centuries.

However different their beginnings, all Lakeland villages have now been touched by tourism. From the crass commerciality of Hawkshead, to simple farm house teas at Kentmere, they're all at it, united by their involvement in the modern tourist industry.

These days millions of visitors pour into the Lake District, desperate to escape the pressures of large towns and cities. Unfortunately, some urban tensions are now being transported to the villages.

Don't worry, this book isn't a deep sociological study. I've tried not to dwell on the political 'hot-potatoes' that afflict rural life. However, they do creep in occasionally.

Nor is it really a guide book. More a celebration that I'd like to share, of some favourite bits of Lakeland. A personal record of a one-man wander through thirty-four villages. Every one I visited was a revelation. Even those I'd known for years had some new things to show me. Only one of them caused me any pain. It seems a small price to pay for such pleasure.

The information I've included is the sort of things I like to know when I go anywhere. A bit of background. What to look out for. If there's a view of mountains, what they are called. You'll find no boring routes round the streets that you have to stick to; these aren't places where you can get lost. Anyway, finding your own way around is part of the enjoyment.

I have included a few walks from village to village, simply because they are conveniently spaced and on foot is the best way to see them. They all have sensational surroundings too.

I'm grateful to my family – Maureen, Tim and Holly for letting me off domestic duties for so long to indulge myself. Their understanding while my mind has frequently been otherwise engaged 200 miles away, has been very touching.

Finally, my thanks to the villagers of Lakeland. All the scenes for my drawings were provided by them. I never heard a cross word from anybody.

I wouldn't take so kindly to a stranger taking photos of MY house.

Jim Watson

Rugby, 1988.

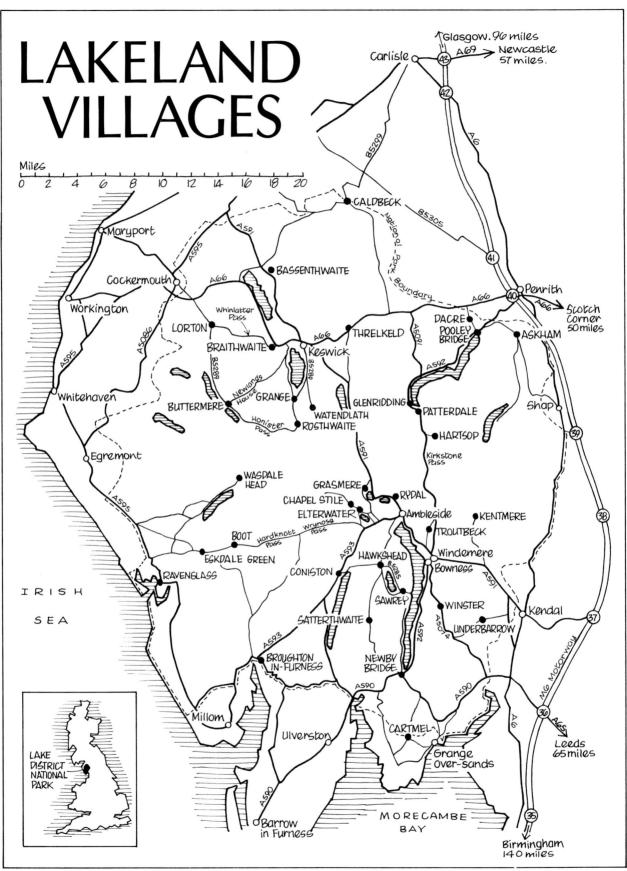

LAKELAND VILLAGES

Miles
0 2 4 6 8 10 12 14 16 18 20

Glasgow 96 miles
A69 → Newcastle 57 miles.
Carlisle
43
42

B5299

B5305

CALDBECK

National Park Boundary

Maryport

A591

A595

A66

A66

41

Bassenthwaite

Cockermouth

Penrith
40

Scotch Corner 50 miles
A66

Workington

A595

A5086

LORTON

Whinlatter Pass

BRAITHWAITE

B5289

THRELKELD

DACRE
POOLEY BRIDGE

A592

ASKHAM

A66

A592

A591

Keswick

Whitehaven

B5289

Newlands House

GRANGE

GLENRIDDING

Shap

39

Egremont

BUTTERMERE

Honister Pass

WATENDLATH

ROSTHWAITE

PATTERDALE

HARTSOP

Kirkstone Pass

A591

A595

WASDALE HEAD

GRASMERE

RYDAL

CHAPEL STILE

ELTERWATER

Ambleside

KENTMERE

38

IRISH

SEA

BOOT

Hardknott Pass

Wrynose Pass

A593

TROUTBECK

Windemere

ESKDALE GREEN

CONISTON

HAWKSHEAD

B5285

Bowness

A591

RAVENGLASS

SAWREY

WINSTER

Kendal

37

SATTERTHWAITE

A5074

UNDERBARROW

A592

A5084

M6 Motorway

BROUGHTON IN-FURNESS

NEWBY BRIDGE

36

A65

Leeds 65 miles

A590

A6

Millom

A5092

Ulverston

CARTMEL

A590

Grange Over-sands

35

MORECAMBE BAY

Barrow in Furness

Birmingham 140 miles

LAKE DISTRICT NATIONAL PARK

Parkin Memorial Hall, Pooley Bridge.

Contents

Askham

Designers of modern housing estates could learn a lot here. As a planned village of space and good looks, Askham has no equal in Cumbria.

After leaving red sandstone-built Penrith, the road south enters limestone country of bleak farmland. Nearer Askham things improve as the woodland of Lowther Park softens the landscape.

I arrived from the south, after travelling 200 miles of rain-soaked M6 motorway. From the exit road at Shap Fell summit, the rest of my journey here was a gentle – though wet – meander through peaceful farmland.

The village has a mile-long single street that runs east to west down a hill between Askham Fell and the River Lowther. It is crossed at mid-point by the Penrith to Haweswater road, where it is possible to park in a small square – if you're lucky.

In 1724 the village was bought by the powerful Lowther family as part of their extensive development of Cumbria. Their influence over the years has cleverly kept Askham a working village, without destroying any of its old-world charm. Many of the modern residents work for Lowther Estates and Land Rovers driven by well-bred chaps in flat hats are a common sight around the village.

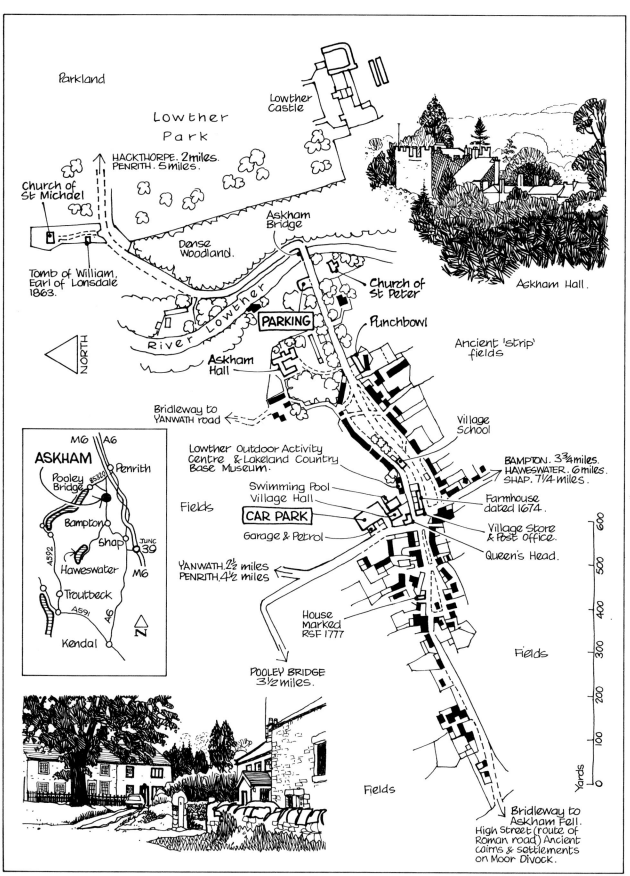

Parkland

Lowther
Park

Lowther
Castle

HACKTHORPE. 2 miles.
PENRITH. 5 miles.

Church of
St Michael

Askham
Bridge

Askham Hall.

Dense
Woodland.

Church of
St Peter

Tomb of William,
Earl of Lonsdale
1863.

PARKING

Punchbowl

Ancient 'strip'
fields

NORTH

River Lowther

Askham
Hall

Village
School

Bridleway to
YANWATH road ←

Lowther Outdoor Activity
Centre & Lakeland Country
Base Museum.

BAMPTON. 3¾ miles.
HAWESWATER. 6 miles.
SHAP. 7¼ miles.

Swimming Pool
Village Hall

Fields

Farmhouse
dated 1674.

CAR PARK

Village Store
& Post Office.

Garage & Petrol

Queen's Head.

ASKHAM

M6 A6

Penrith

Pooley
Bridge

B5320

Bampton

Shap

JUNC
39

A592

Haweswater

M6

YANWATH. 2½ miles
PENRITH. 4½ miles

600

A6

500

Troutbeck

A591

House
marked
RSF 1777

400

N

Fields

300

Kendal

POOLEY BRIDGE
3½ miles.

200

100

Fields

Yards

0

Bridleway to
Askham Fell.
High Street (route of
Roman road) Ancient
cairns & settlements
on Moor Divock.

9

The village centre.

The limestone-built houses and farms of Askham are lined-up facing each other across a series of village greens. Door and window surrounds of each sturdy building has its own tasteful colour of paint. Some have tiny front gardens, but many doors open directly onto the pavement. All the buildings are well cared-for, most date back to the early 18th century.

Green Croft, a pleasant modern estate of terraced houses around a green, makes an interesting comparison to the older version.

Rain still poured down so I dripped into the Queen's Head, dated 1682. In the genteel lounge well-dressed patrons were eating pub lunches. The only person wearing walking boots and a bright orange anorak was me.

I left to shelter in the post office instead. It's bright and cheerful, but the only tourist information I could find were a couple of ancient picture postcards.

Brightening skies saw me heading up the hill, between groups of

attractive buildings. Some look onto a central green, others face downhill for the view.

Towards the top of the village the road becomes a lane where old farm buildings have been converted to dwellings and close-cropped lawns added. The lane continues onto the fell to wander between the mounds of ancient burial grounds.

Returning downhill, I found the drab village hall next to the Queen's Head. Next door the public swimming pool shone as the sun came out. Outdoor swimming in chilly Cumbria seems a bit daring, but this isn't the only village where it goes on!

A small cottage nearby is burdened by the title of 'Lowther Outdoor Centre and Country Base Museum', across its front door. It was closed, but apparently this rather odd place is a store house of information about Askham life.

Over to my right I caught a first startling view of Lowther Castle, rising theatrically from the distant woodland. At this point the village green is so wide, being nosey about a neighbour living opposite would require the use of strong binoculars.

A terrace of three cottages makes an attractive picture with the huge trees of Askham Hall as a background.

The Village Green and Lowther Castle

Standing to one side of the lowest green is the white-painted Punchbowl Hotel. Judging by the folks I saw coming and going, this is the pub the locals use.

Beneath three magnificent copper beech trees, the road steepens to enter the densely vegetated gorge of the River Lowther. Hot sunshine was now making the wet trees and shrubs steam. St John's Church was an amazing sight, rising like an ancient temple from a humid, tropical jungle.

Farmhouse dated 1674.

The Earl of Lonsdale, the 7th in line of the Lowther family to hold the title, lives at the Hall. Though private and well-screened by trees, it can be seen from a lane near the entrance. Much of the building is 14th century, embattled parapets and turrets still remain.

Originally built for the Sandford family, Askham Hall has been described as 'spacious, but not grand'. It looked pretty grand to me.

Up the hill to the west.

Terraced cottages near Askham Hall.

The Punchbowl.

I crossed the swollen, brown river into Lowther Park where there is a church of a much different world, at the top of the hill.

St Michael's was built in 1832 by Robert Smirks, who had also designed Lowther Castle, 25 years earlier. His church is mock Norman in style. The ostentatious Gothic arches, columns and furnishings were more, I suspect, to the glory of the Lowthers rather than that of the Almighty.

At the entrance to the churchyard the Gothic tomb of William Lowther stands – as dramatic as the set of a Hammer horror film.

St John's is an austere church with a stone-flagged floor, no stained glass and a serious damp problem. A wooden gallery high in the east end looks down on a bleak altar. The Sandfords of Askham Hall built the south transept sometime before the 16th century, for use as a family burial chapel.

Then during the 19th century, the old building was demolished and a new church was built on the original ground plan. The south transept, still with its 1661 stone font was dedicated as a baptistery in 1950.

The Queen's Head.

St. John's Church.

Down some dank, stone steps a marble effigy of the noble Lord can be seen, frozen forever behind thick glass. A great patron of the arts, William died in 1863. He had an interminable poem dedicated to him by Wordsworth, whose family were supported by four generations of Lowthers.

Throughout Cumbria, the Lowther family is legendary. James, the first Earl of Lonsdale, brought the industrial revolution to his West Cumbrian coalfields where he built most of the town of Whitehaven.

St Michael's Church.

Lowther Castle was built between 1806 and 1811. Even in semi-ruin it is a remarkable sight. The size of the vast ballrooms can easily be imagined and the many turrets and towers are reminiscent of a fairy-tale castle. Eventually every fairy-tale reaches 'The End', when the real world returns. Within the ravaged walls of Lowther Castle the Earl now keeps his chickens.

Leaving Askham, I took the road sign-posted 'Celleron' towards Pooley Bridge. Quite unexpectedly, a tremendous view appeared. The Pennines, Penrith, and the broad plain of the River Eamont were all laid out before me. It was a moment to stop and savour. There had been many that day at Askham.

From 1880 to 1944 the title was held by the fifth Earl, Hugh. He did much to empty the family coffers, but little to bring in any money at all. A great sportsman, he left the famous Lonsdale belts for boxing as one of his bequests. The colour yellow was another strange passion. Cars, servants, and the Automobile Association, of which he was their first president, had to be decked out in yellow.

The 'Yellow Earl' was last of the Lowther big spenders, leaving huge debts on his death and the family seat, Lowther Castle, in sad disrepair. Without money for repairs the decline was irreversible. In 1958 the castle was partly demolished to the façade we see today.

James, the present Earl, is an astute businessman and the Lowther Estates are again profitable.

Mausoleum of William, Earl of Lonsdale. 1863.

Lowther Castle.

13

Central village and Skiddaw

Bassenthwaite

When the popular tourist spots have become too packed for pleasure, it's good to know there are places like this. Snuggled in behind Skiddaw and missed by main roads, Bassenthwaite is a haven of peace and normality.

I like to go by the road to the north of the lake crossing the fine stone bridge over the River Derwent and passing a clutch of posh hotels and guest houses. Near the Castle Inn, on the narrow road to the village, there's a fine view of the fells across Bassenthwaite Lake. A grand panorama, from Sale Fell at the northern entrance to the Lake District, to the wild crags of Borrowdale away in the south.

Nearer the village the huge mass of Skiddaw grabs the attention. A curving ridge leads up to Ullock Pike, along Longside Edge and on to the barren summit. Enclosed within are the mysterious valleys of Barkbethdale and Southerndale. A beautiful sight in a sunset. The mountain is the fourth highest in Lakeland and Skiddaw slate is some of the oldest rock in Europe.

North of the village a wooded hillside rises to the desolate Uldale Fells and the lonesome tarn of Overwater. Bassenthwaite is sheltered on three sides and looked quite cosy to me.

Bridge over Dash Beck.

14

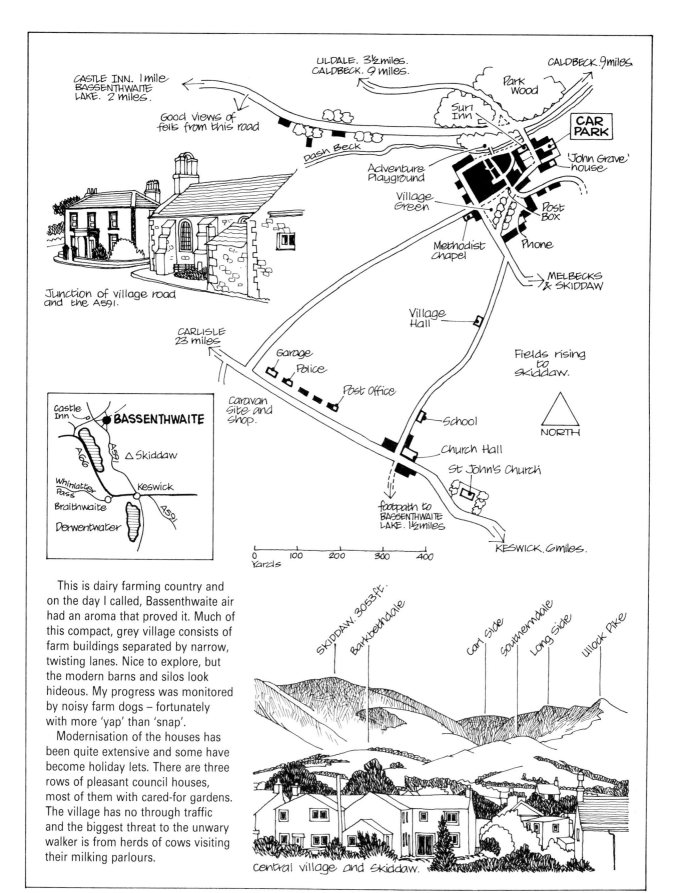

ULDALE. 3½ miles.
CALDBECK. 9 miles.

CALDBECK. 9 miles

CASTLE INN. 1 mile.
BASSENTHWAITE
LAKE. 2 miles.

Park
Wood

Sun
Inn

CAR
PARK

Good views of
fells from this road

Dash Beck

Adventure
Playground

'John Grave'
house

Village
Green

Post
Box

Phone

Methodist
chapel

MELBECKS
& SKIDDAW

Junction of village road
and the A591.

CARLISLE
23 miles

Village
Hall

Fields rising
to
Skiddaw.

Garage

Police

NORTH

Castle
Inn

BASSENTHWAITE

A591

△ Skiddaw

A66

Whinlatter
Pass

Keswick

Braithwaite

A591

Derwentwater

Post Office

Caravan
site and
shop.

School

Church Hall

St John's Church

footpath to
BASSENTHWAITE
LAKE. 1½miles

KESWICK. 6miles.

0   100   200   300   400
Yards

This is dairy farming country and on the day I called, Bassenthwaite air had an aroma that proved it. Much of this compact, grey village consists of farm buildings separated by narrow, twisting lanes. Nice to explore, but the modern barns and silos look hideous. My progress was monitored by noisy farm dogs – fortunately with more 'yap' than 'snap'.

Modernisation of the houses has been quite extensive and some have become holiday lets. There are three rows of pleasant council houses, most of them with cared-for gardens. The village has no through traffic and the biggest threat to the unwary walker is from herds of cows visiting their milking parlours.

SKIDDAW. 3053ft.

Barkbethdale

Carl Side

Southerndale

Long Side

Ullock Pike

Central village and Skiddaw.

15

Cottages by village green.

'John Grave's' house.

The only amenity is the Sun Inn. A friendly pub serving good food and my favourite Lakeland brew of Jennings Bitter. Years ago an enterprising landlord built the stone bridge to give coaches access to his hostelry.

Two miles upstream the Dash Falls are an exciting sight. but the beck flows more sedately through the village. I had a pleasant stroll by the stream, and was surprised to find a farm-house selling stone troughs, and an adventure playground for children, properly built amongst the trees.

A few fields away the rest of the village straggles alongside the A591, once the coaching route from Keswick to Carlisle. A couple of modern semis house the police and the post office. The village hall is sited well away from any houses, perfect for noisy local hops.

Bassenthwaite boasts two churches. St John's is closest to the village and was finished in 1878. Fairly big, with an apse, it has an inappropriate, pencil-shaped spire. Sprawling yew trees complete a rather depressing picture.

The village green is not of the pretty variety, with broken-down goal posts and bald patches in the grass, but it does have a formal avenue of trees and some old cottages in a corner.

Up the hill towards Skiddaw the modern village craft of motor body repairs appeared to be thriving in a small domestic garage.

Nearby, I was struck by an imaginative garden and a plaque which stated, 'This house done by John Grave. 1776'. Many hands must have 'done' it since then because the house looks quite modern now.

Church of St John the Evangelist.

Sun Inn.

Worship at this spot goes back to 7th century St Kentigern and the beginnings of religion in the north of England. The atmosphere of primitive myth remains. Tennyson, who used to stay at nearby Mirehouse, is said to have been inspired to write his famous lines about Excaliber while walking here. As dusk settled over the dark waters of the lake I could well believe it.

The forestry people have done a very successful landscaping job on the fells to the east of Bassenthwaite Lake, removing their objectionable fir trees to reveal the natural lines of the hills.

Spectacularly situated though it is, the lake does not draw hoards of visitors. Much of the shore is given over to nature conservation and the water is little used by the general public, apart from anglers and yachtsmen.

As I returned to the road the setting sun caught the tops of Dodd and Skiddaw, flashing kaleidoscopes of colour above the dark trees. I hadn't seen anybody for hours.

Twenty minutes later I was back in Keswick, which was teeming with people. Five minutes more and I was missing Bassenthwaite.

St Begas' church occupies a lonely site in meadows close to Bassenthwaite Lake, which can only be reached on foot. The track was muddy and I was thankful not to be in a funeral cortège or dressed for a fine wedding.

Norman in origin, this is the perfect parish church in miniature. It has a bell-tower like a school, and inside, a 12th century chancel arch. Wordsworth, local arbitor of good taste, worshipped here with his lake poet cronies. I found it spotlessly clean, with shining brass and lots of fresh flowers.

Coming upon this lovely place unlocked and unprotected against a society hellbent on destroying any kind of peace and beauty, moved me deeply.

St Bega's church.

The village and Harter Fell.

Boot

How does a place set in one of the loveliest of Lakeland valleys get such an apparently derogatory name?

The question turns out to be more interesting than the answer. 'Boot' is no more than a corruption of the Middle English word for 'a bend in the valley'.

Eskdale is a typical U-shaped glacial valley stretching the eight miles from the high central fells, down to the coastal plain at Ravenglass. Boot is about one quarter of the way down, tucked away by the rocky outcrop of Great Barrow.

Rich deposits of haematite were found on both sides of the valley. Nab Scar mine was opened in 1870 and houses were built for the miners. Boot (and boots) had set foot in Eskdale.

In 1870 a 3 foot gauge railway was finished to take the haematite down to the main line at Ravenglass. Two years later the price of iron ore collapsed. The company was in trouble but Boot mine struggled on until closure in 1912. During the next three years the railway was replaced by a 15 inch gauge catering for the first tourists. Despite some ups and downs it survived, and now a ride on 'la'al Ratty' is a popular and picturesque way to visit Boot.

Cottage near Corn Mill.

18

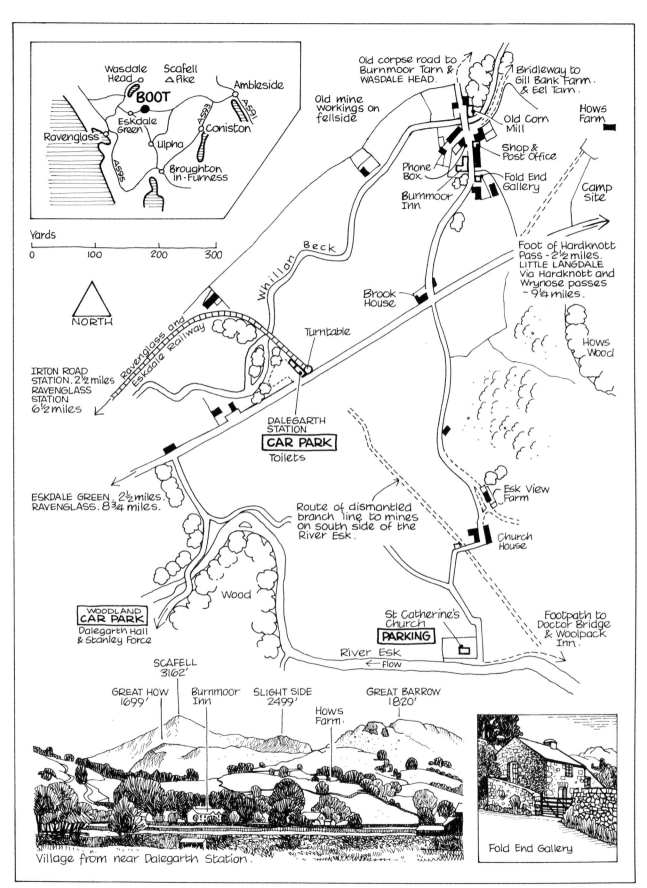

Wasdale
Head
Scafell
△ Pike
Ambleside
BOOT
Eskdale
Green
Coniston
Ravenglass
Ulpha
Broughton
in-Furness

Old corpse road to
Burnmoor Tarn &
WASDALE HEAD.

Old mine
workings on
fellside

Bridleway to
Gill Bank Farm.
& Eel Tarn.

Hows
Farm

Old Corn
Mill

Shop &
Post Office

Phone
Box

Fold End
Gallery

Burnmoor
Inn

Camp
Site

Yards

0   100   200   300

Whillan Beck

Brook
House

Foot of Hardknott
Pass - 2½ miles.
LITTLE LANGDALE
Via Hardknott and
Wrynose passes
- 9¼ miles.

Hows
Wood

NORTH

Ravenglass and Eskdale Railway

Turntable

IRTON ROAD
STATION. 2½ miles.
RAVENGLASS
STATION
6½ miles

DALEGARTH
STATION
CAR PARK
Toilets

ESKDALE GREEN. 2½ miles.
RAVENGLASS. 8¾ miles.

Route of dismantled
branch line to mines
on south side of the
River Esk.

Esk View
Farm

Church
House

Wood

**WOODLAND
CAR PARK**
Dalegarth Hall
& Stanley Force

St Catherine's
Church
PARKING

River Esk
← flow

Footpath to
Doctor Bridge
& Woolpack
Inn.

SCAFELL
3162'

GREAT HOW
1699'

Burnmoor
Inn

SLIGHT SIDE
2499'

Hows
Farm

GREAT BARROW
1820'

Village from near Dalegarth Station.

Fold End Gallery

There are walls here that are five feet thick. Not to keep in a Rambo-like breed of sheep, but because this was a way the early farmers could get rid of all the stones that littered the valley floor.

In the lane to the village, I went past Brock House, a guest house that's into survival courses, where wet weather walking gear danced on the washing line like orange can-can dancers. Opposite the comfortable and old Burnmoor Inn, a line of flash cars were parked outside a row of modest miners' cottages. Holiday lets, I concluded.

The post office is basic but cheerful in the front room of a main-street semi. Nearby, is a 15th century corn mill that had been long disused when it was restored in 1975 and opened as a working tourist attraction.

I crossed the pack horse bridge over Whillan Beck and was surprised to find myself climbing the fellside. Was that it? Surely that baby's booteeful of buildings that I had just seen at a glance couldn't be the 'capital of Eskdale'? Boot really was once an important metropolis. Where I was standing, pack horse trails had crossed, the corpse road to Wasdale had begun and the railway from the coast had ended.

And what a view. Clear across the green valley to Harter Fell. Clad in bracken lower down, a belt of heather higher up, then topped by a crown of clean-cut ramparts of rock. A beautiful mountain.

Reversing my tracks along the single Boot street, I went down a quiet lane to St Catherine's, the 17th century parish church of Eskdale. The simple, local granite building has a solitary position on the bank of the River Esk. In the churchyard there's an impressive headstone for Tommy Dobson, much-admired Master and founder of the Eskdale foxhounds.

The river looked lovely, with deep, silent pools among patches of pebbles, where the water flowed faster, sparkling in the sunshine.

Main Street.

The Old Corn Mill.

Burnmoor Inn.

Esk View Farm

St. Catherine's Church.

I had a look at the remains of a bridge just upstream, that used to carry the railway to the mines. Then I travelled the final three miles east to the dalehead.

Eskdale is not very fertile, and grazing of the land by sheep goes way back. Brotherilkeld, Eskdale's remotest farmstead, was owned by Furness Abbey during the 12th century.

The only road out of the valley head is Hardknott Pass. A sensationally steep climb. One-in-three in places and quite hair-raising in modern traffic. Almost unbelievably, this twisting test for today's vehicles was once a Roman road. The remains of a walled fort stand overlooking the valley on a spectacular site nearby. It was built in the first century AD as part of a chain of garrisons across Cumbria to reinforce the Roman occupation.

Looking down the length of Eskdale to the ghostly towers of Sellafield nuclear plant always strikes me as being truly the sublime to the ridiculous. Man survives in the dale by treating nature with respect, abusing her atomic structure could have disastrous results.

This had been my first walk through Eskdale. I hope it's not my last.

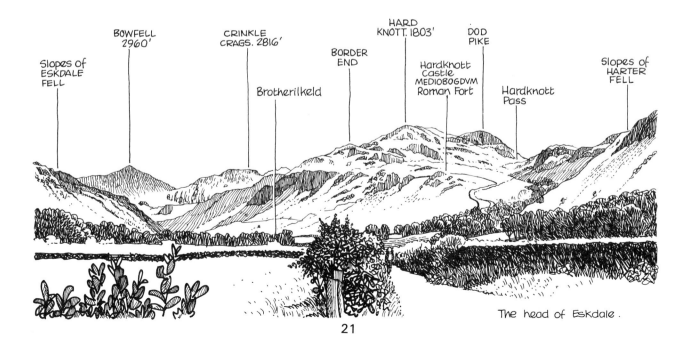

The head of Eskdale.

21

Coledale Beck & Central village

Braithwaite

The building of a three lane highway through the northern lake district was much criticised by conservationists, but the A66 does give motorists some attractive views of the fells between Keswick and Braithwaite.

There's Catbells, like the back of a dozing camel, then a glimpse up Newlands behind tree-covered Swinside, to Causey Pike with the humps, and Barrow, the gravel heap. Proud Skiddaw is across the swampy fields to the right, and ahead there's Barf with its famous white-painted Bishop Rock. Braithwaite is pushed into the fells like a wedge and almost overlooked.

This is a village of great variety which makes it seem bigger than it really is. There are three distinct areas, modern houses to the north, plusher properties south of the beck, and an old central core. Many a pleasant surprise turns up just around the corner.

Very much a holiday place, the whole gamut of accommodation plies for trade here. But this is not Butlins, and local folk accept tourism on their terms only. Braithwaite has been rewarded by many awards in 'Best kept village' competitions.

Old village and slopes of Grisedale Pike.

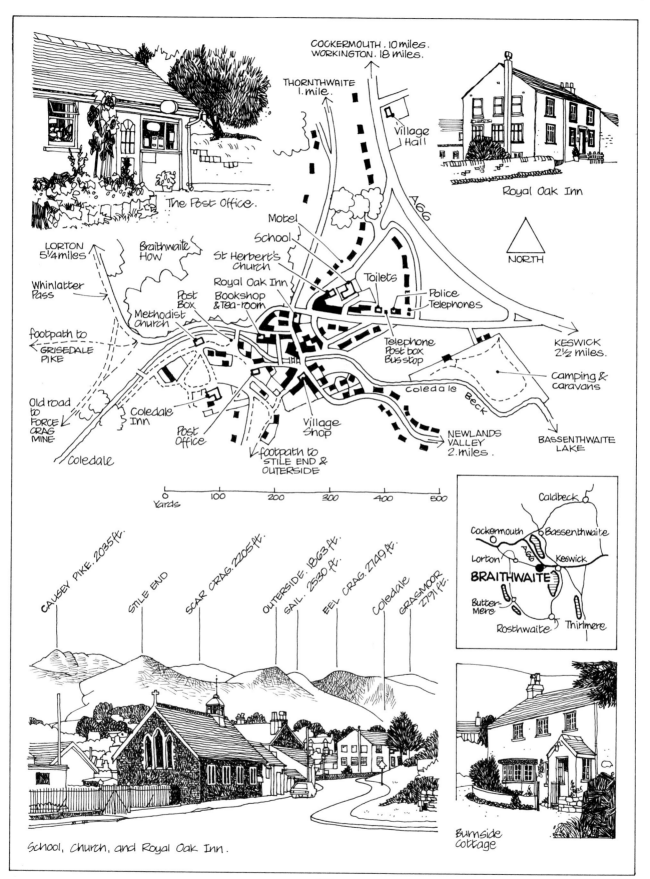

The Post Office.

Royal Oak Inn

COCKERMOUTH . 10 miles.
WORKINGTON . 18 miles.

THORNTHWAITE
1. mile.

Village Hall

A66

NORTH

LORTON
5¼ miles

Braithwaite How

Motel

School

St Herbert's Church

Toilets

Royal Oak Inn

Whinlatter Pass

Post Box

Bookshop & Tea-room

Police
Telephones

Methodist church

footpath to
GRISEDALE PIKE

Telephone
Post box
Bus stop

KESWICK
2½ miles.

Old road to
FORCE CRAG MINE

Coledale Inn

Coledale Beck

Camping & caravans

Post Office

Village Shop

NEWLANDS VALLEY
2 miles.

BASSENTHWAITE LAKE

Coledale

footpath to
STILE END &
OUTERSIDE

Yards   100   200   300   400   500

Caldbeck

Cockermouth   Bassenthwaite

Lorton   A66   Keswick

BRAITHWAITE

Butter-Mere

Rosthwaite   Thirlmere

CAUSEY PIKE. 2035 ft.

STILE END

SCAR CRAG. 2205 ft.

OUTERSIDE. 1863 ft.

SAIL. 2530 ft.

EEL CRAG. 2149 ft.

Coledale

GRASMOOR. 2791 ft.

School, Church, and Royal Oak Inn.

Burnside Cottage

For such a pretty village the pub and the church are disappointing. Though old and attractive inside, the Pack Horse looks very plain, and the Coledale Inn is far too remote. St Herbert's church has no churchyard and is dedicated to the Derwentwater hermit. It was built in 1900 to replace an old mission room and still looks remarkably like a mission room.

In summer the narrow streets around the shop get jam-packed with the cars, boats and boots of many holiday makers.

cottages by main road.

The Cumberland Pencil Company began in Braithwaite, moving to new premises in Keswick after a fire in 1898.

Barytes used to be dug at Force Farm mine at the head of Coledale but the village has no legacy of mining, apart from workers' cottages. Coledale Beck babbles briskly between the houses, little wooden bridges being the only way to reach some front doors. Outerside rises right in the village and the lower slopes are planted with daffodils amongst the paths.

'The Old Farmhouse'. Dated 1656.

Village shop.

Braithwaite How is an outcrop of Grisedale Pike that hides Whinlatter Pass like a secret. It's a steep climb up into Thornthwaite Forest, that passes a much-admired view over Bassenthwaite Lake on the way. At the foot of the pass there's an interesting little tea-room cum bookshop in a barn near the bridge.

From a picnic place just upstream, the steepness of Grisdale Pike looks very daunting. The Pike is one of a horseshoe of fells which encloses Braithwaite. All six rugged summits can be visited on a splendid walk – the Coledale Round. I have yet to tread the famous nine miles, being content to just sit and stare over my sandwiches.

Across the valley there's an even greater show as the classic sculpture and magnificent bulk of Skiddaw is seen full on, making a colourful and dramatic sight. At Braithwaite the guest houses line the hillside like boxes at the opera.

This village is a mixture of architectural styles, from 17th century farmhouses to green-slate bungalows and terraced council houses. But it all seems to gel into an interesting, friendly and cared-for place that's always a pleasure to visit. I will continue to call.

Royal Oak, Stanger House & Braithwaite How.

Bridge at foot of Whinlatter Pass.

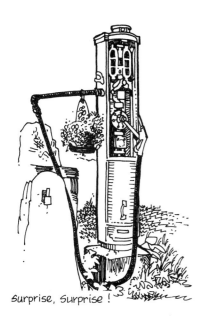

Surprise, Surprise!

Miners' cottages.

25

The Old King's Head.

Broughton-in-Furness

Purists may say this is neither 'Lakeland' nor 'Village'. Broughton is near the sea and does feel like a town, but it is also just in the National Park, only seven miles from Coniston lake and with a population much less than that of Grasmere. So it does qualify for this book. Besides – village or town – I like it.

The A5092 had brought me here. A roller-coaster of a road which crosses the tail-end of many a Lakeland valley. Broughton is at the end of Dunnerdale, where the estuary of the River Duddon cuts deep into Cumbria.

A settlement was recorded here in the 12th century and markets have been held since 1593. Merchant ships used to sail into the estuary to trade for coppice wood cut from the fellsides. Locally-spun wool fed the mills of Yorkshire. Broughton grew to a prosperous market town, but with the growth of heavy industry during the Victorian era, businessmen turned to the iron and steel towns of Millom and Barrow, leaving this a town in size only.

The sheep market has survived, and with the growing popularity of the Duddon Valley, Broughton is finding a new role in the tourist industry.

The Square

26

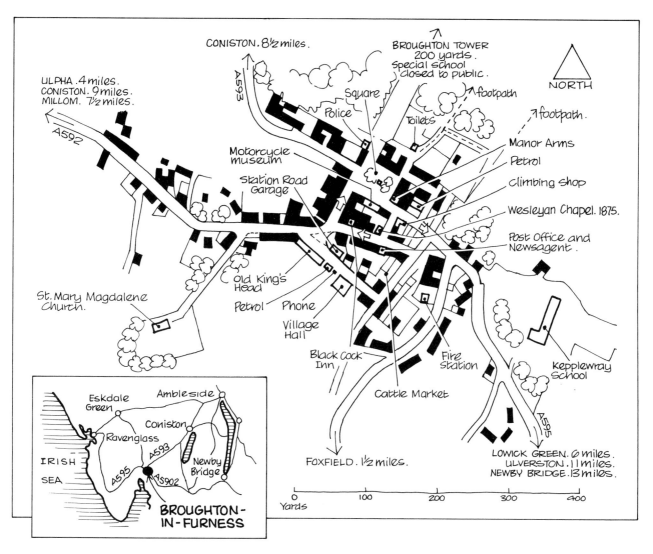

CONISTON. 8½ miles.

BROUGHTON TOWER
200 yards.
Special school
closed to public.

NORTH

ULPHA .4 miles.
CONISTON. 9 miles.
MILLOM. 7½ miles.

A592

A593

Square

Police

footpath

footpath.

Toilets

Manor Arms

Petrol

Climbing shop

Motorcycle museum

Station Road Garage

Wesleyan Chapel. 1875.

Post Office and Newsagent.

St. Mary Magdalene Church.

Old King's Head

Petrol

Phone

Village Hall

Black Cock Inn

Cattle Market

Fire Station

Kepplewray School

A595

Eskdale Green

Ambleside

Coniston

Ravenglass

A593

Newby Bridge

IRISH SEA

A595

A5902

BROUGHTON-IN-FURNESS

FOXFIELD. 1½ miles.

LOWICK GREEN. 6 miles.
ULVERSTON. 11 miles.
NEWBY BRIDGE. 13 miles.

0   100   200   300   400
Yards

CORNEY FELL   THWAITES FELL   ULPHA FELL

The Village from near Kepplewray School.

27

There's a one-way traffic system through the village which has to cope with heavy traffic using this busy West Cumbria supply route. Most of the streets are on hills, often rich in carbon monoxide fumes.

The terraces of old buildings are of dark grey Coniston granite, which enhances the feeling of being a town. Fortunately, nature keeps breaking through with views of the Ulpha Fells, Black Combe, and the distant Duddon Sands.

I parked in the large square, centre and focal point of the village. Terraced houses, a rather nondescript pub, the old Town Hall, a pretty restaurant, and a pleasant tea-room line the edges. It was developed to generous Georgian proportions at the end of the 18th century by John Gilpin Sawrey of Broughton Tower, after he had seen the squares of London.

The Old Town Hall.

The three-storey formal houses are aging quite well but some – like those of London – have been converted to flats. An amusing weather-vane tops the striking old Town Hall but the clock looks as though it was added on as an afterthought. The series of arches that once held shop fronts now hides a snooker hall. Upstairs is 'Jack Hadwin's Motorcycle Museum'. An enthusiast's collection of old machines found locally and put on show for bikers of all ages to drool over. A bit unusual for a Georgian square, but Broughton is like that.

Up Coniston Road some new houses were being built, but I was far more taken by the exuberant Gothic style of the slate house across the road.

Within a few more steps the 'town' had melted away and I was in the countryside.

Old saw mill.

House on Coniston road.

Houses in the square.

Just down the road there's a climbing shop. Proof again that Broughton isn't too far from the fells. Indeed the ebullient proprietor behind the counter was togged out ready to scale Scafell at anytime.

Along a back street I was astonished to find a gleaming Grand Prix racing car in a stone shed. The body shell had been removed and the monster, all aluminium struts, tyres and engine, was being worked on. I never saw the mechanic, but fondly imagine him to look just like the TV character in 'Last of the Summer Wine', with oily blue overalls, round glasses, and a flat cap, worn back to front.

Returning down the hill I admired the glorious chestnut trees in the square. A new wooden seat hugs one that shades the old stocks and some curious rock slabs, once reputedly used to sell fish.

Nearby is the stark obelisk whose stepped base makes a handy platform for the local youngsters to drape themselves round. A plaque tells us that it was erected in 1810 to commemorate the 50th year of the reign of King George the third.

Every August the square is the setting for a quaint little ceremony when the Lord of the Manor reads out Broughton's ancient charter and throws pennies for the children. The present Lord is Lancashire County Council who sportingly send along a representative to do the reading, toss away 50p's worth of pennies and then repair to the Manor Arms for sherry and biscuits. Councils are often accused of wantonly throwing away money but this seems to me to be both thrifty and eminently worthwhile.

Despite being a bustling car park, it is easy to linger in the square. But I had much more to see.

Obelisk, stocks, and fish slabs in the square.

Approach from Lowick Green.

Lower Syke House on Ulpha road.
Marked 'ADE 1655. Rebuilded by CNH 1740'.

The railway branch line from Foxfield to Coniston ran through the wooded cutting at the bottom of the hill, until 1958. A row of railwayman's houses still gaze-out sadly on what is no more. Broughton Station has been converted into a couple of unusual homes subtly incorporating the railway architecture. The sidings are now a housing estate where it's interesting working out where the lines used to go.

Farm-stock feed suppliers are still here and the market continues. But my visit was soon after the movement of stock in Cumbria had been severely restricted due to the Chernobyl nuclear disaster, and the sheep pens were all silent.

I climbed the hill to Kepplewray School and stopped to chat to an old chap who was tending a garden nearby. Done it for 50 years he said, for all the people who had lived in the house. He was also one of the 30 swill-makers who used to work in the village. Swills are large blister-shaped baskets woven out of strips of wood, mostly used by farmers for collecting crops. Making them used to be a substantial industry in this area.

Cottages near the Square.

Black Cock Inn.

In the lane to the church, a disused school has been turned into solid looking houses. Interestingly, Kepplewray School, across the village, was once a large house.

St Mary Magdalene's looks a bit forbidding. The site was consecrated in 1547, but the central core is late Norman. In 1874 the north aisle was added and the tower erected in 1900.

The clock carries a dire warning in large gold lettering, 'Watch, for ye know not the hour'.

The main street is lined by cheerful shops. Small business mainstays of market town life. A post office and newsagent, a grocer, confectioner, and chemist. And a pub of course. The Black Cock Inn, door flung wide to the street.

Across a square, chaotic with cars, stands the Old King's Head, washday white and regal.

Just down the road, the village hall is high-roofed and substantial. Beyond it I could see the church, glowering at the houses from a hollow amongst the open fields.

Church of St. Mary Magdalene.

Broughton Tower.

Broughton Tower is a spacious mansion built around a 14th century pele tower and hidden from the village by large trees. This was once the home of the Sawrey family, powerful Puritan folk who, almost alone amongst the local gentry, supported Cromwell during the civil war.

The Tower is now a special school and closed to the public. It can be seen from a public footpath, but I was disappointed by the medley of architectural styles.

Broughton is a splendid, out of the ordinary sort of a place, full of quirky character and interest. I had come expecting a sleepy market town but had discovered much more.

The village and Mellbreak

Crag Farm. A traditional early 17C farmhouse.

Buttermere

My father was fond of saying, "There's nowt but scenery at Buttermere." He was almost right. The mountains are so imposing here, the handful of buildings huddle together like children frightened by domineering parents.

The Buttermere valley is eight miles long, running north-west from the high ground around Great Gable. The tiny village is between two lakes, Buttermere and Crummock Water.

From Cockermouth the road is flat but the change from a landscape of gentle pastureland is dramatic. More adventurous motorists have a choice of two passes. Newlands valley is delightful on foot but a drag in a car. Coming down the steep hause, Buttermere and the lake are hidden until the final corner. The most popular and exciting approach is over Honister Pass from Borrowdale, where the road plunges down a ravine of such devastation that it's a relief to reach the tranquility of the lake.

The relative inaccessibility of Buttermere suits selfish types like me who want to hog it all for themselves. I've yet to see a coach party here, but those ubiquitous mini-buses are a creeping menace.

32

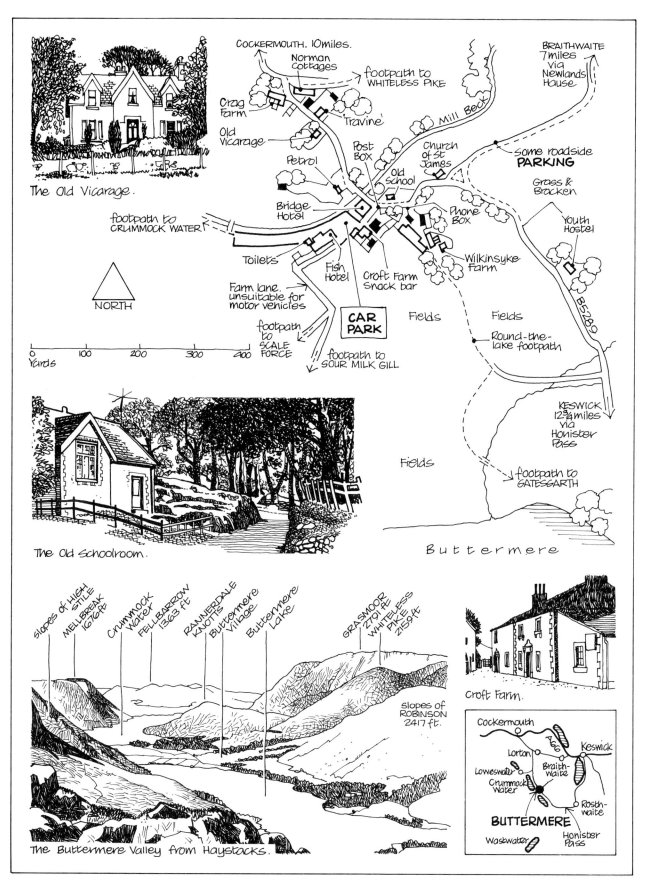

The Old Vicarage.

NORTH

0   100   200   300   400
Yards

The Old Schoolroom.

Map labels:

COCKERMOUTH. 10 miles.

Norman Cottages

footpath to WHITELESS PIKE

BRAITHWAITE 7 miles via Newlands Hause

Crag Farm

'Travine'

Mill Beck

Old Vicarage

Petrol

Post Box

Church of St James

some roadside **PARKING**

Bridge Hotel

Old School

Grass & Bracken

footpath to CRUMMOCK WATER

Phone Box

Youth Hostel

Toilets

Fish Hotel

Croft Farm Snack bar

Wilkinsyke Farm

Fields

Fields

B5289

Farm lane. unsuitable for motor vehicles

CAR PARK

Round-the-lake footpath

footpath to SCALE FORCE

footpath to SOUR MILK GILL

Fields

KESWICK 12¾ miles via Honister Pass

Fields

footpath to GATESGARTH

Buttermere

The Buttermere Valley from Haystacks.

slopes of HIGH STILE
MELLBREAK 1676ft
Crummock Water
FELLBARROW 1363 ft
RANNERDALE KNOTTS
Buttermere Village
Buttermere Lake
GRASMOOR 2791 ft
WHITELESS PIKE 2159ft
slopes of ROBINSON 2417 ft.

Croft Farm.

Cockermouth
A66
Keswick
Lorton
Loweswater
Braithwaite
Crummock Water
Rosthwaite
BUTTERMERE
Wastwater
Honister Pass

Buttermere hardly qualifies as a village, but all the year round swarms of people congregate here filling the extensive car park to overflowing. Roadside parking even creeps up the hill by the church. Tut-tut, most unsightly. If you see a parking space at Buttermere, grab it fast. You may never see another all day.

Most of this area belongs to the National Trust who impose strict controls on any development. Buttermere has no new buildings, most date back to the early 17th century. The Bridge Hotel shows a smart country-house side to the main road, while around the back, boot-shod crowds are served beer and filling food.

During 1805 the Fish Hotel became famous throughout the country. Mary Robinson, daughter of the landlord, was tricked into marriage by a bigamist and con-man who called himself, the Honourable Alexander Hope. He was unmasked by the local gentry, tried for forgery and hanged at Carlisle a year later. 'No-Hope' Mary, had songs and plays written about her and nosey folk came to ogle the 'Beauty of Buttermere'. Now the Fish Hotel is a similar tourist attraction standing forlornly in the middle of a car park.

Bridge Hotel.

Fish Hotel.

Church of St. James.

The tiny church was built in 1840 on a rock perch above the village. Twin bells hang in the bell turret and the wrought iron porch gate depicts a hill shepherd and his sheep.

Inside there's fine woodwork and items donated by faraway fans of the valley. Sixteen carved angels gaze down from the ceiling, finding much to praise.

34

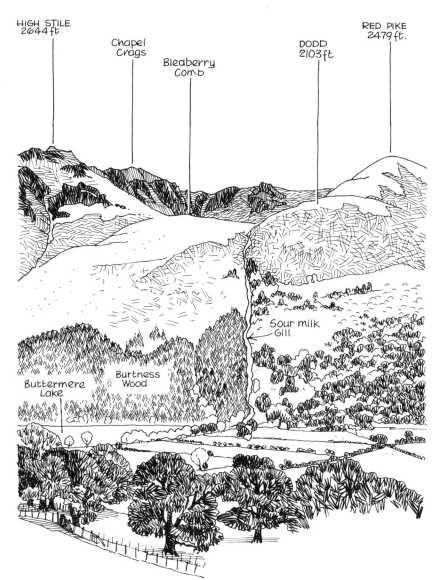

HIGH STILE
2644ft.

Chapel
Crags

Bleaberry
Comb

DODD
2103ft.

RED PIKE
2479ft.

Sour milk
Gill

Burtness
Wood

Buttermere
Lake

In my opinion, the finest family walk in all of the Lake District is the four miles around Buttermere lake. No need for a map, just follow the crowds. The path goes through Wilkinsyke Farm, a typical Lakeland sheep farm with a splendid bank barn in the corner of the yard. A bit further on, there's a tunnel through the rock which was dug by gardeners from Hassness House to give them something to do in the winter.

At 94 feet, the lake is quite deep by Cumbrian standards. Lack of organic material keeps the water very clear. The only sediment comes from Honister slate quarries, giving the magnificent reflections a unique greenish quality. Trout fishing is good, but most visitors walk, climb or just point cameras.

Buttermere village, though still very pleasant, is becoming a huge car park and it is memories of the fabulous fells that linger longest.

Aye, there's almost nowt but scenery here.

Up the hill towards Cockermouth a fine, slate-built house has traditional corbie-stepped roof gables. Nearby Crag Farm and Norman cottages make an attractive grouping.

But here it's the fell scenery that dominates, and across a few fields there is the most imposing sight of all. A wall of volcanic rock rises straight out of the lake to a skyful of summits – High Stile, High Crag and Red Pike. Water cascades down Sour Milk Gill from Bleaberry Tarn, hidden away in a lofty basin. Buttermere has many fine fells, but they shrink at the sight of these awesome neighbours.

Norman Cottages. Named after John Norman, an early resident who sailed on HMS Bounty.

Caldbeck

Village centre.

Most people know this area as being the hunting ground of John Peel, prolific hunter of foxes, but there's much more here to remember.

Like Back o' Skiddaw. Mist-soaked moorland, crossed straight and unfenced, by the lonely road from Bassenthwaite. Or the approach through Mungrisedale, just as moody, where Blencathra seems to go on forever. Even the road to Carlisle climbs to a memorable view-point across the Solway Firth before dropping down into the village.

Caldbeck lies in a limestone basin, with tree-covered hills to the north and brooding Blencathra away in the south. There's a great sense of space with wide streets and small, bright cottages. Extensive doing up of places was going on, but I was surprised to find no new buildings of any kind.

Although a few farms skirt the streets, and fields surround the village, this doesn't seem to be an intensive farming area. Indeed, the visitor may ponder, as I did, why a settlement of this size is here at all.

A small community sprang up around the church, but it was during the 18th and 19th centuries that there was the most spectacular growth. Caldbeck grew to an important industrial and mining boom-town with a population of 1500. And with thirteen ale-houses, a wild and woolly place it must have been!

Now a peaceful home for 700 folk, the village gives a fascinating look-back to those days and some proof that there can be life after industrial decline.

Gatesbridge.

Bottom of Ratten Row. House on left used to be The Wheatsheaf Inn.

36

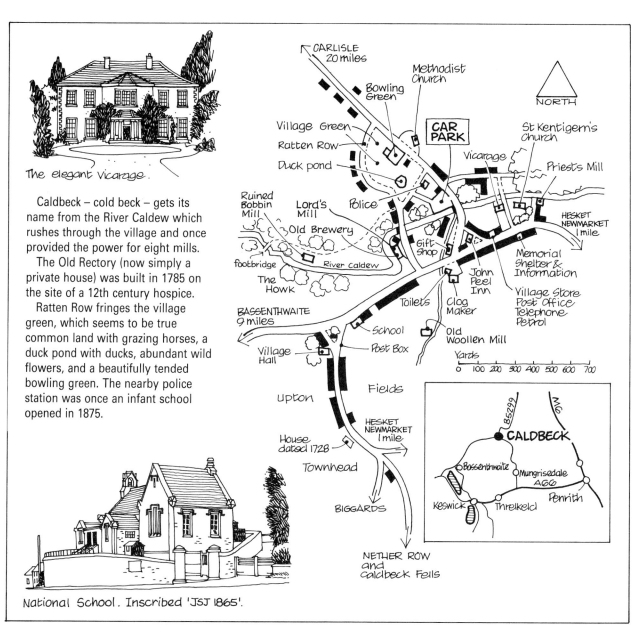

The elegant Vicarage.

Caldbeck – cold beck – gets its name from the River Caldew which rushes through the village and once provided the power for eight mills.

The Old Rectory (now simply a private house) was built in 1785 on the site of a 12th century hospice.

Ratten Row fringes the village green, which seems to be true common land with grazing horses, a duck pond with ducks, abundant wild flowers, and a beautifully tended bowling green. The nearby police station was once an infant school opened in 1875.

National School. Inscribed 'JSJ 1865'.

Riverside.

The duck pond and police station.

37

John Peel was born in 1776 at Parkend, near Caldbeck. He married the daughter of a well-off farmer who bore him 13 children. Family man he wasn't and spent most of his time hunting or singing popular ditties in the pub.

In 1829, one of his boozing pals, John Graves, wrote some words about Peel that they sang to a popular Scottish folk tune. Graves owned the local woollen mill which had produced the heavy cloth of Peel's 'coat so grey'. A year later Graves left his wife to lead the life of a ne'er-do-well in Tasmania, where he died in 1886.

Peel died of a hunting accident in 1854 and thousands of people turned out for his funeral. His ornate headstone can be seen to the left of the church door.

William Metcalf, who was the choirmaster at Carlisle cathedral, gave the song a new tune in 1869 and after being sung in London, *D'ye Ken John Peel* became a big hit.

The words were first sung in the bar of what is now called the John Peel Inn. Considering the characters of Peel and Graves, the previous name – 'The Oddfellows' – seems far more appropriate.

John Peel Inn and Gate House, home of John Graves, is across road on left.

The Shelter. Built to the memory of Peel and Graves.

The church and River Caldew.

St Kentigern's Church.

The church was built about 1140, where St Kentigern had preached in 553AD. Basically Norman in style, it has been added-to and modified over the years. A friendly church, the venue for a Bring and Buy Sale on the day I visited.

The churchyard has the graves of J. Peel and that of Mary Harrison, better known as Mary Robinson, the Beauty of Buttermere. After her humiliation by the dastardly Hope, Mary found happiness with a Caldbeck farmer.

Lord's Mill, with a checker-brick mill-town chimney, was grinding corn in 1704. It was rebuilt in 1830 and used as a mill until 1914.

The building next door was a wheat mill dating back to 1670, but by 1810 it had become a brewery, slaking the thirsts of the local workers. Brewing ceased with the industrial boom, at the end of the 19th century.

Just upstream, I found the ruins of the bobbin mill, with a date stone of 1857 and two beautifully arched doorways. The wood drying shed is in good condition, but the 42 feet diameter water wheel, once the largest in Britain, was scrapped for the war effort in 1940. At one time 60 men and boys worked here. Final closure came in 1920.

Negotiating the old walls, I climbed between the trees, grown tall since the demise of the bobbin makers, and entered 'The Howk'. Here the river has formed a spectacular gorge in the limestone, with two deep holes, The Fairy Kettle and The Fairy Kirk, where the water spins and froths with agitation.

The romantic Victorians loved to come here for large, organised picnics, and the local paper would carry reports on the weather. I saw not a soul, it was pouring with rain, but the river in full spout was obligingly dramatic.

The Woollen Mill was built a few fields away in 1862 and employed 20 hands. It still stands and is now a private house and engineering business. Local farmers used to smother their sheep in a mixture of tar and grease, so before it could be dyed the wool had to be cleaned, or 'fulled'. This was done underneath the cobbler's shop of today, then dyed in the building of the present gift shop.

Priest's Mill was built in 1702 by the rector who also built the church tower in 1727. Last used as a sawmill, it is now a restaurant and craft workshops.

Since Elizabethan times, the Caldbeck Fells have been extensively mined, mainly for silver, copper and

Brewery and Lord's Mill with the chimney

Ruined Bobbin Mill in The Howk.

lead. Digging out the ore must have been punishing enough, but the 18th century miners also carried it across ten miles of bleak fellsides to be smelted at Keswick. Eventually, all the seams were exhausted, although the final mine held out until 1965.

Coal was dug in the village itself, from shallow pits on Ratten Row, keeping the Caldbeck firesides warm for nearly a century.

This prosperous industrial past is reflected in some of the fine buildings in the village. Mill owners' houses are easily picked out. I find a visit to Caldbeck is interesting on all kinds of levels.

House near Lord's Mill, dated 1690.

The village square.

Cartmel

Like thousands before me, I had come here to see the priory church. Everything else was a bonus.

I motored over knobbly hills from Grange-over-Sands, a pleasant, Victorian sea-side town with an unusually mild climate, to the rather bleak valley of the River Eea.

Cartmel is situated on a peninsula that separates the vast sandy estuaries of the Kent and the Leven. This is another of the villages built on the belt of limestone that skirts the Lake District. Houses and road-side walls are of the white-grey rock that exudes harshness and poverty.

This area was first colonised by Norwegian settlers who built themselves self-contained farmsteads. Many of these manor-houses remain to the north of Cartmel, with today's bewildering maze of roads once the tracks which linked them.

A church and small community existed in the 7th century at Allithwaite, near Cartmel, and this was given to St Cuthbert by the King of Northumbria for the establishment of a monastery. However, it was not until 1190 that a powerful Baron,

William Marshall, Earl of Pembroke, provided a large area of land for the foundation of a priory of Augustine Canons.

Building began on an uninhabited site next to the River Eea. Following a familiar pattern, a village sprang up and Cartmel had begun. The construction of the great church was a huge drain on the resources of the valley and it was the best part of a

century before the transept and choir were finished.

Over the years, a great variety of buildings have been built around the church attracting many admiring visitors.

I parked on the racecourse – a great eye-opener after negotiating country lanes and the narrow and congested streets through the village.

The village and Priory from main car park

40

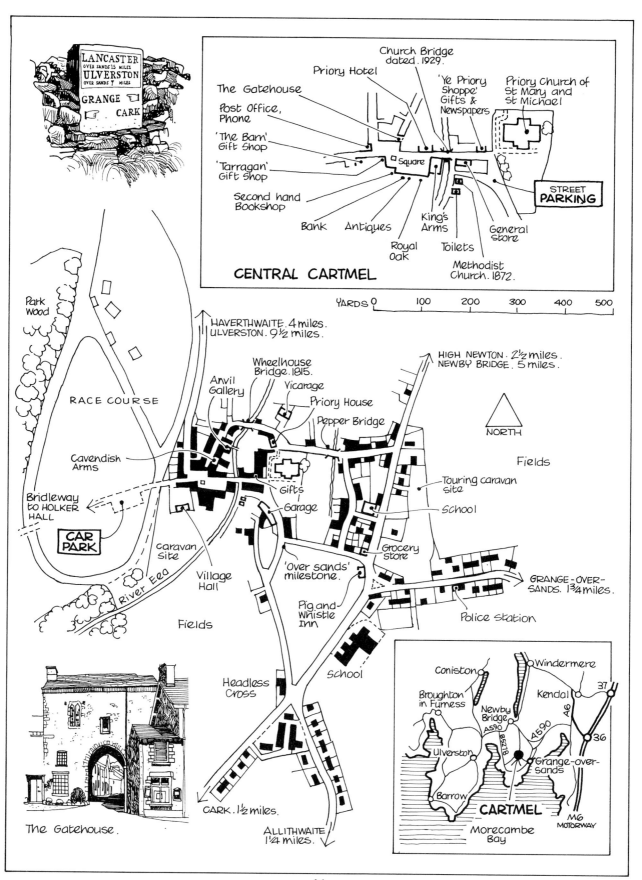

LANCASTER
OVER SANDS 15 MILES
ULVERSTON
OVER SANDS 7 MILES
GRANGE
CARK

CENTRAL CARTMEL

Church Bridge dated 1929.
Priory Hotel
The Gatehouse
Post Office, Phone
'The Barn' Gift Shop
'Tarragan' Gift Shop
Second hand Bookshop
'Ye Priory Shoppe' Gifts & Newspapers
Priory Church of St Mary and St Michael
STREET PARKING
Square
Bank
Antiques
King's Arms
General Store
Royal Oak
Toilets
Methodist Church. 1872.

YARDS 0   100   200   300   400   500

Park Wood

HAVERTHWAITE. 4 miles.
ULVERSTON. 9½ miles.

HIGH NEWTON. 2½ miles.
NEWBY BRIDGE. 5 miles.

RACE COURSE

Wheelhouse Bridge. 1815.
Anvil Gallery
Vicarage
Priory House
Pepper Bridge

NORTH

Fields

Cavendish Arms

Touring caravan site

Gifts

School

Bridleway to HOLKER HALL

CAR PARK

Garage

Grocery store

GRANGE-OVER-SANDS. 1¾ miles.

caravan site

Village Hall

'Over sands' milestone.

Police station

River Eea

Fields

Pig and Whistle Inn

Headless Cross

School

CARK. 1½ miles.

ALLITHWAITE 1¼ miles.

The Gatehouse.

Coniston
Windermere
Broughton in Furness
Newby Bridge
Kendal
37
A590
A6
Ulverston
A590
B5278
Grange-over-Sands
36
Barrow
M6 MOTORWAY
CARTMEL
Morecambe Bay

The Square.

Church Bridge.

The Village Hall.

Every village in England seems destined to have a gift shop in a barn selling the same woollen goods, baskets, pottery and prints, in the same pot-pourri atmosphere. I passed by the Cartmel example and entered the square.

A collection of pubs, fine houses, a bank, antique shop, second-hand book shop, and another lookalike gift shop, are lined-up around a battered pencil-stub of an obelisk and a rickety, old village pump. Grouped on a slope, the feeling is not of enclosure, but of the buildings falling away.

The top end looks the best, with the gable end of the post office prominent among the ivy-clad houses. Some are ancient and stooped, others tall and elegant.

Parked cars blight the square and pose the perpetual questions; ban them completely and create a museum piece, or restrict parking to just a little eye-sore? Cartmel seems to have got the balance between practicality and aesthetics about right. If only people would obey yellow-line regulations!

42

Cavendish Street.

the Lake Artists' Society, only slightly less impressive than the gatehouse itself.

A high archway led me into Cavendish Street with its smart Georgian terrace, the oldest inn in Cartmel, a huddle of cottages, and the Helen Bradley Centre.

In 1966, and at the age of 60, Mrs Bradley moved to Cartmel and began to paint. She produced a large body of work and several books. Her naive paintings of Lancashire life before the 1914-18 war are very popular, and up to 20,000 visitors tour The

Cavendish Arms and Gatehouse.

Dominating this part of Cartmel is the Gatehouse, pitted and scarred like the face of an ancient warrior. It was built around 1330, as the entrance to the priory precincts. Now it is the last remnant of the walled cloisters. Originally the upper room was a manorial courtroom, followed by a variety of uses – grammar school, refuge for poor families, methodist chapel and warehouse.

In 1946 it was given to the National Trust, who didn't seem to know what to do with it either. Today it houses a permanent exhibition of paintings by

Grange-over-Sands road.

43

Helen Bradley Centre each year. Sadly, I have yet to be included in the count. On both my visits the centre was closed.

The Priory Church of St Mary and St Michael is a huge barn of a building. No product of text book architecture this, but true design-as-you-build vernacular style.

Construction began in the 13th century when the core of the church was established.

In 1410, the belfry tower was added to the low lantern tower in the freakly unique diagonal position that has amazed architects ever since. About the same time, the nave was built, as cheaply as possible. A look at the pieces of stone used show them to be much more crudely hewn than the rest of the walls.

Cartmel priory was destroyed in 1537 on the orders of King Henry the Eighth. The gatehouse was spared, and after some nifty appeal negotiations, the church was saved on the grounds that it was being used for parish worship.

Unfortunately, the roof and windows had already been removed and for 80 years, the Cumbrian elements carried on the destruction the King had begun.

Then in 1610, George Preston of Holker Hall came to the rescue and began a 13 year restoration, for which we should all give thanks.

When Roundhead soldiers stabled their horses in the nave in 1643, indignant local folk shot at them, leaving bullet holes (still to be seen) in the door at the south west corner. Traces of lead were found in the door in 1955.

The interior of the church is spacious and astonishingly beautiful. Round, dog-toothed arches border the choir and above, elegant triforium arches cross the delicately mottled white stone walls. A memorable carved screen surrounds the choir stalls and under the seats there are misericords of animals and birds. The 15th century east end window, with original stained glass, is 45 feet high and most impressive.

I stayed for quite a while, enjoying the knick-knacks displayed around the walls and taking-in the tranquility of this very special place.

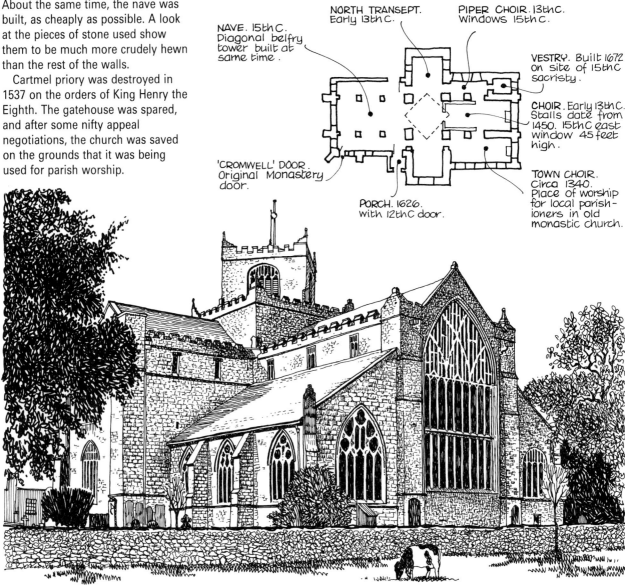

NORTH TRANSEPT. Early 13th C.

PIPER CHOIR. 13th C. Windows 15th C.

NAVE. 15th C. Diagonal belfry tower built at same time.

VESTRY. Built 1672 on site of 15th C sacristy.

CHOIR. Early 13th C. Stalls date from 1450. 15th C east window 45 feet high.

'CROMWELL' DOOR. Original Monastery door.

TOWN CHOIR. Circa 1340. Place of worship for local parish-ioners in old monastic church.

PORCH. 1626. with 12th C door.

The Priory Church of St. Mary and St. Michael.

44

Cartmel used to be a natural resting place for the fishermen and cocklers working their way across the treacherous Morecambe Bay sands. Just down the road from the church, a stone gives the distances across the sands to Lancaster and Ulverston. On no account attempt these walks!

The narrow street next to the church was packed with excited pensioners who told me they had walked over the hills from Grange. 'Ye Priory Shoppe' – shame about the name – was busy. As were the general store and a plain but serviceable tea room.

I returned to the racecourse to have a look round this remarkable attraction so close to the village streets.

Racing on this site was documented in 1856, but some claim that the priory monks raced mules here in the 16th century. Steeplechase meetings are now held around the May and August Bank Holidays.

The organisers pride themselves on being 'professional amateurs', and have been rewarded with crowds of up to 15,000 people. The course is used for many sporting events and rallies, Cartmel Agricultural Show was being set-up while I was there.

Rose Cottage.

The Racecourse.

The racecourse is leased from nearby Holker Hall, a great friend to Cartmel and a magnificent 17th century stately home, drawing many visitors to the house and motor museum. Prone to a bit of show-biz razzamatazz, but well worth a visit, if only to walk round the wonderful gardens.

Cartmel village has two other parts, quiet and rather ordinary, to the west and south.

I must admit, I was a bit disappointed with Cartmel. Everything I'd read or been told had gone-on about how lovely it is. Individual houses are, but taken as a whole, the jumble of different styles makes a tour of the village a bit like a walk through a classy, but badly organised, furniture store.

What I'd really come to see was the priory church, and that had amply made-up for any minor disappointments.

45

Chapel Stile

For a village set in probably the busiest bottleneck in the Lake District, Chapel Stile is amazingly peaceful and unspoilt.

The main road just misses the village, seeming to almost push it out of the way and up the craggy fellside. This road from Ambleside is a scenic delight all the way, but pulses quicken when Chapel Stile is reached and the first inviting view of the Langdale Pikes is seen.

Thousands of buses, vans, cars, motor-bikes, cycles and walkers charge up the road, anxious to reach the delights of Great Langdale. You'd think it was going to be closed-down any minute! Not as fanciful as it might seem. There have been suggestions that the Langdale valley should have restricted access, to reduce overcrowding and erosion. That would probably turn Chapel Stile into a giant car park and 'facility support centre', which doesn't bear thinking about.

Meanwhile, Chapel Stile sits beside the main road, like an old fellow on the village seat, shaking his head in disbelief as the crazy world rushes by.

The two villages of Elterwater and Chapel Stile must have almost been one when the slate quarries and gunpowder factory were in full production. Now with quarrying much reduced and the sprawling time-share estate an alien barrier between them, they are separate and different in character.

46

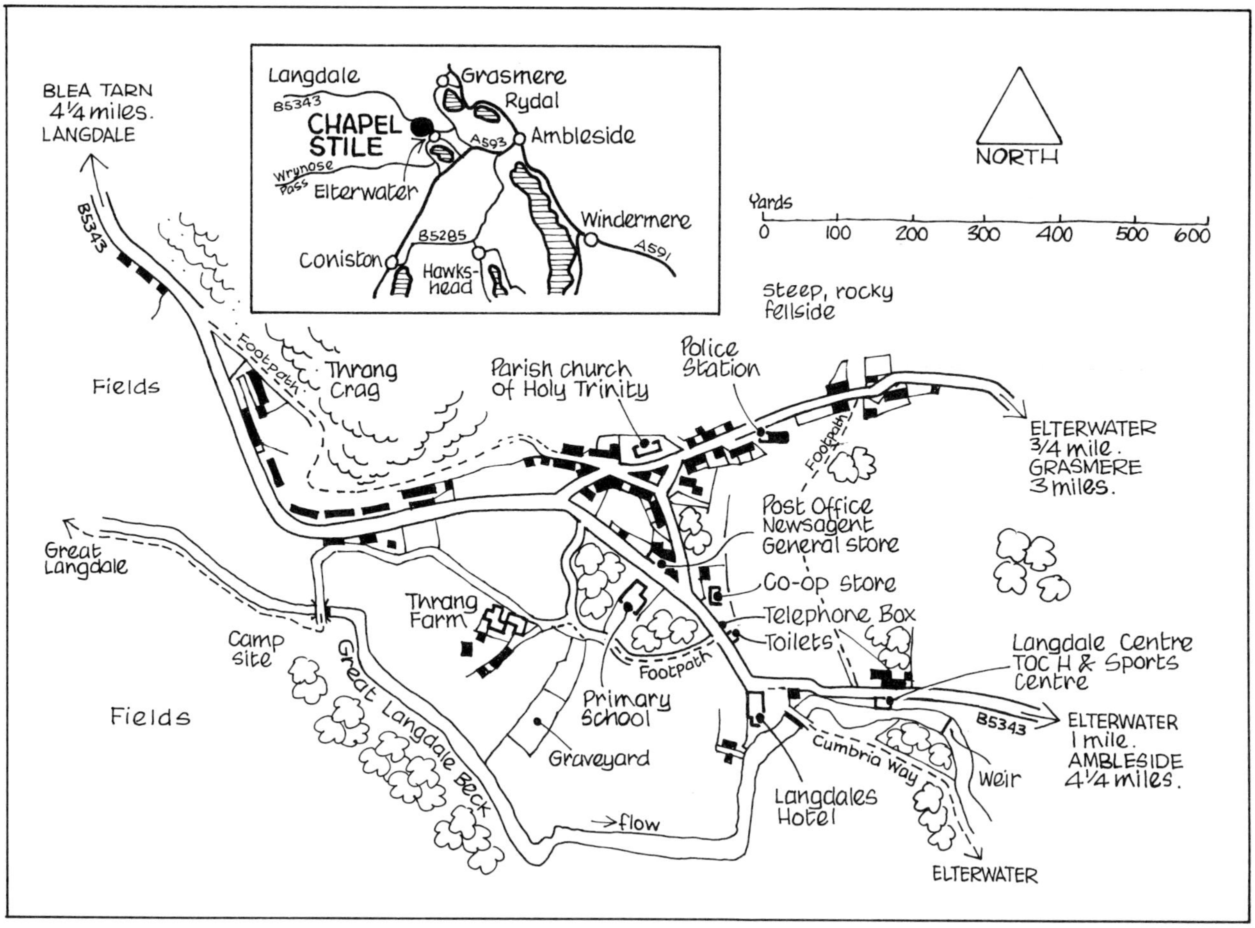
BLEA TARN
4¼ miles.
LANGDALE
B5343
Langdale
B5343
CHAPEL STILE
Wrynose Pass
Elterwater
Grasmere
Rydal
A593
Ambleside
B5285
Coniston
Hawks-head
Windermere
A591
NORTH
Yards
0
100
200
300
400
500
600
Steep, rocky fellside
Fields
Footpath
Thrang Crag
Parish church of Holy Trinity
Police Station
ELTERWATER
¾ mile.
GRASMERE
3 miles.
Footpath
Great Langdale
Post Office
Newsagent
General store
Co-op store
Telephone Box
Toilets
Thrang Farm
Camp site
Footpath
Primary School
Langdale Centre
TOC H & Sports Centre
Fields
Great Langdale Beck
Graveyard
B5343
ELTERWATER
1 mile.
AMBLESIDE
4¼ miles.
Cumbria Way
Weir
Langdales Hotel
flow
ELTERWATER

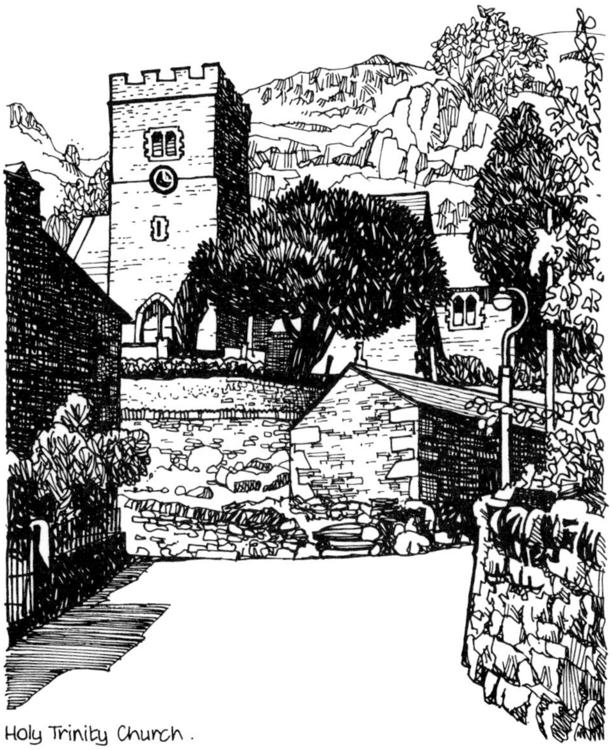

Holy Trinity Church.

Parking in the village is well-nigh impossible. Wherever you stop it's somebody's way. I left my car at the roadside and scurried away before anyone linked the obstruction with me.

The Langdale Hotel is a fine looking place with large gardens going down to the river. An extension, with 'Wainwright's Bar' emblazoned across it, was packed with people, and I wondered what the grand old man – no lover of crowds – made of the honour the hotel has done him.

I turned the corner and was again struck by the remarkable setting of this village. Slate-built cottages climb up the steep fellside which is broken by outcrops of rock, ledges of close-cropped grass, banks of bracken, and patches of colourful heather. A huge and perfect rock garden, much imitated on a domestic scale.

Holy Trinity church stands highest of all the buildings, on a wide ledge supported by a tall and substantial slate wall. Quite a large church with no windows on the side next to the fell. The style is early 14th century, but it was built in 1857 to replace a chapel of 1750. There's fine views from the churchyard and a row of idyllic Lakeland cottages by the gate. On the street below, a 1887 water fountain commemorates the golden jubilee of Queen Victoria.

The oddly-shaped post office is a cluttered and friendly place, selling anything and everything with a cheery bit of chat. Local folk and a dog lazed outside in the sunshine questioning the sanity of passing sweaty hikers. Two petrol pumps are long dry, but seem to have been left as a fiendish joke to confuse motorists.

Just up the road are some new houses. Large and expensive looking, but blending very well with the old.

Post Office and village stores.

The slate-built terraced cottages are delightful. Some had high-powered, 'Yuppy' sports cars parked outside, but others had their doors wide open with stout, ruddy-faced ladies in pinnies chatting on the doorsteps. An old chap in boots, waistcoat, tie, flat cap and fluffy, white moustache, ambled by, pushing a wheelbarrow while sucking an old pipe. Down south, they'd pay £5 a time to see this sort of a scene acted out in a 'living museum'.

Cottages near church.

Climbing between old cottages and along the fellside, the back road makes a splendid scenic walkway to Elterwater.

I paused amongst pecking hens and took in the view from a grassy bank. The sound of blasting had clattered between the hills and it was gratifying to see how well the quarries merge into this naturally wild and shattered landscape. Over Lingmoor Fell, the large and isolated range of Coniston fells shimmered in the haze.

Back road to Elterwater.

Unlike the straight troughs of other Lakeland valleys, Great Langdale has an unusual twisting form. This was caused by glacial ice being diverted by a powerful fault in the volcanic rock near what is now Chapel Stile. Further erosion and weathering over millions of years created the familiar crags and scree slopes of Langdale.

Neolithic man took advantage of this breaking down of the rock and fashioned axe-heads from shattered pieces picked up from the fell gullies. Many discarded stone axes have been found on Pike o' Stickle and archaeologists have established that this was one of the most important manufacturing sites in the country.

From near Thrang Farm.

The village from the south east.

An unobtrusive path took me to Thrang Farm and a sensational sight. As if from a fragile present, soft tissue paper mist was lifting to reveal the Langdale Pikes in awesome detail. Their much-loved profile – like two huge stone lions in repose – is recognizable from miles away. No visitor to Chapel Stile should leave without seeing this dramatic, close-up view.

Great Langdale scenery is spectacular but it does lack a lake. Blea Tarn does its best, up a steep little road at the head of the valley and can be quite memorable on the right day.

Chapel Stile is a grand place, pretty in places with a good sense of community. Most of the houses fit into the setting very well, but the three rows of modern houses on the Langdale side of the village are a much-criticised disaster. With all the planning authorities the Lake District has, it is baffling how something like this can be allowed to happen.

Langdale Pikes & Thrang Farm. (Cumbria dialect, 'Thrang' = busy).

Yew Pike and Black Bull Hotel.

Coniston

All roads to Coniston go through wonderful countryside. Gentle and pastoral from the south; rugged, undulating and wooded from the north.

The village is large, bitty, and not very pretty, so arrival can seem like an anti-climax. But the situation between Coniston Water and the Coniston Fells is superb and the elevated streets command good views of the lake.

Two main streets are lined by large slate buildings with Victorian shop fronts and living accommodation upstairs. Just like Keswick or Ambleside. In fact Coniston was all set to grow to their size, when local industry collapsed leaving the village in a state of limbo that still persists.

However, this is right on the Lakeland coach trip circuit and many visitors regularly wander the streets. Ice cream stalls and cafés seem to do well and the pair of very good inns have plenty of outside tables.

I visited during an invasion of cackling Lancashire pensioners, wise-cracking themselves into a right old state of merriment. They would've found no tourist centre glitz here, everything is old-fashioned and a bit frayed at the edges. It does have an honest charm though, and the old folks certainly enjoyed it.

Cottage at Dixon Ground.

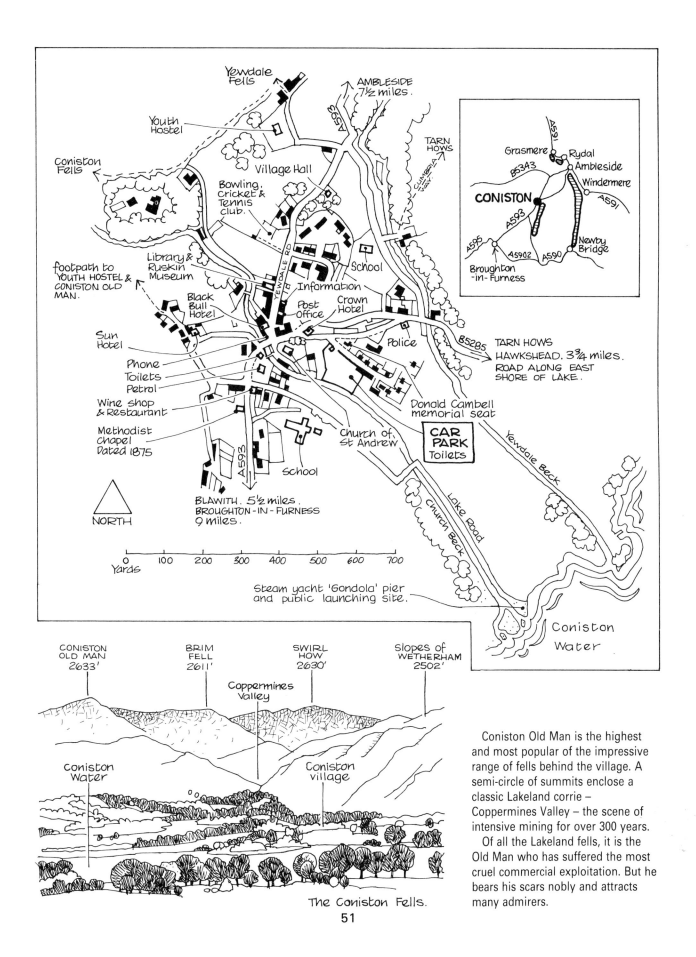

Yewdale Fells

Youth Hostel

Coniston Fells

AMBLESIDE 7½ miles.

A593

TARN HOWS

CUMBRIA WAY

Village Hall

Bowling, Cricket & Tennis club.

Library & Ruskin Museum

footpath to YOUTH HOSTEL & CONISTON OLD MAN.

Black Bull Hotel

Information

Post Office

Crown Hotel

School

YEWDALE RD

Sun Hotel

Phone
Toilets
Petrol

Wine shop & Restaurant

Methodist Chapel Dated 1875

A593

School

Police

Donald Cambell memorial seat

B5285

TARN HOWS HAWKSHEAD. 3¾ miles. ROAD ALONG EAST SHORE OF LAKE.

CAR PARK Toilets

Yewdale Beck

Church Beck

Lake Road

Church of St Andrew

NORTH

BLAWITH. 5½ miles. BROUGHTON-IN-FURNESS 9 miles.

0   100 200 300 400 500 600 700
Yards

Steam yacht 'Gondola' pier and public launching site.

Coniston Water

Grasmere Rydal
A591
B5343 Ambleside
CONISTON Windermere
A593 A591
A595 A5902 A590 Newby Bridge
Broughton-in-Furness

CONISTON OLD MAN 2633'

BRIM FELL 2611'

SWIRL HOW 2630'

Slopes of WETHERHAM 2502'

Coppermines Valley

Coniston Water

Coniston village

The Coniston Fells.

Coniston Old Man is the highest and most popular of the impressive range of fells behind the village. A semi-circle of summits enclose a classic Lakeland corrie – Coppermines Valley – the scene of intensive mining for over 300 years.

Of all the Lakeland fells, it is the Old Man who has suffered the most cruel commercial exploitation. But he bears his scars nobly and attracts many admirers.

51

Tilberthwaite Avenue.

The Village Hall

Copper mining began here in the 16th century, reaching a peak output about 1860. For nearly 80 years the lake was a busy waterway, bringing iron ore to be smelted in the many lakeside bloomeries fed by wood from the local forests. Slate quarries were opened on the Old Man and at Tilberthwaite, attracting even more workers to the village. In 1859 the mines were linked to the main coastal railway by a branch line to Foxfield.

But the big-time didn't last. Mining companies who had hoped to find gold and silver as well as copper, pulled-out and a steady decline set-in. By 1890 mining had virtually ceased. The railway line was not popular with tourists and was closed-down in 1957.

Yewdale Road leads to a more open and prettier part of the village, with an estate of bungalows and a fine games field. The village hall is very striking, with a pagoda-like porch worthy of the approval of John Ruskin himself.

Crown Hotel

The Black Bull was once a coaching inn where the painter Turner stayed in 1797. An awkward bridge crosses Church Beck, gurgling happily for me, but it has been known to rise rapidly and burst its banks causing much flooding.

Shops are of the market town, butcher – grocer – baker variety, with a refreshing absence of barn-type gift shops. Old barns are a bit hard to come by here. Coniston Co-op, however, takes up half the street.

Part of the village institute is the Ruskin Museum, a collection of rather pitiful objects that once belonged to John Ruskin. So typical of the woefully inadequate way the great man is commemorated. But 10,000 people a year visit the museum, so that can't be bad.

St Andrew's church was built in 1819, on the site of a chapel that William Fleming of Coniston Hall had built in 1586. A chancel and vestry was added in 1891 when the church was completely restored. But it's a dull, grey-stone building, rather uninteresting, and surrounded by huge fir and yew trees.

Yewdale Road.

A local man who died in 1963 won the VC and is remembered by a special stone in the churchyard war memorial.

John Ruskin died at Brantwood in 1900 and was buried here in preference to Westminster Abbey.

His grave carries a florid Anglo-Saxon type cross carved from local Tilberthwaite green slate.

St. Andrew's church.

Ruskin's Grave

53

Coniston railway station used to be situated up a steep hill near the 16th century Sun Hotel Inn. As I sweated my way upward it became clear why the position was so unpopular with voluminously-skirted Victorian ladies. An alley next to the inn leads to Dixon Ground Farm, a fine picture set against Yew Pike.

There's little of the station to see now, but its elevated position is amazing. Even higher up the hillside, the terraced houses have a marvellous view over the lake.

Coniston Water is about five miles long, half a mile wide and over 180 feet deep at the southern end. The two small islands were made the setting of 'Swallows and Amazons', by Arthur Ransome, who lived at the lakeside.

This lake – quiet as a mere in a rich man's park – shot to national prominence in January 1967 when Bluebird, a jet-propelled boat piloted by Donald Campbell, back-flipped and sank while attempting to break the world water speed record. Campbell was never seen again. The large stone seat in the village is a sedentary memorial to a man dedicated to speed.

Sun Hotel.

'Gondola'.

Dixon Ground Farm.

The steam boat 'Gondola', has a story as romantic as her looks. Furness Railway Company built her in 1856, and she was in continuous service on Coniston until 1919. Then she was used as a boat house until blown ashore one stormy night and left to rot. After being sold for scrap in 1966, she was resold to an admirer who managed to refloat the hull after three years' hard work.

A National Trust appeal then raised £250,000 for a complete renovation, and since her relaunch in 1980 Gondola has carried up to 86 passengers a trip, up and down the lake in considerable luxury.

54

Brantwood.

John Ruskin. (1819-1900)

treasures and Ruskin memorabilia. Recently, a Wainwright collection has been added to give more popular appeal. A bit sad really. If only Ruskin had stuck to one thing. Wrote a few lines about daffodils maybe . . .

Across the lake from Brantwood the 15th century cruck-framed Coniston Old Hall was being restored by the National Trust. Four enormous, round chimneys make the Hall a landmark for miles around, and remind me of Battersea Power Station. Is that why London-born Ruskin liked the view so much?

I'd never been overfond of Coniston, but after poking about a bit and finding much of interest, my feelings towards the village had warmed appreciably.

John Ruskin was an austere and remarkable man whose influence on English life is disgracefully under-valued. An artist, writer, critic and philosopher, he spent a fortune trying to help the poor. He was a co-founder of the National Trust, but also made another very noticeable contribution to the look of the area: the neo-gothic style of the buildings in many Lakeland towns – and Coniston – is directly attributable to his influence.

Ruskin bought Brantwood in 1871 for the view across the lake, and without seeing the house. He spent the last thirty years of his life turning it into a flamboyant mansion. Brantwood now attracts 20,000 visitors a year to see the art

Coniston Old Hall in course of restoration and across the lake, Brantwood and Grinedale Forest.

Dacre

If there was a league table of the most visited Lakeland villages, Dacre – pronounced Day-ker – would come well down the list. It's on the road to nowhere, away from all bus routes, and without famous fell or lake. There's frugal amenities and no place to park a car. So why was I filled with eager anticipation as I headed for this back of beyond place?

The answers were to be clearly seen as I descended the hill into the tiny village: an ancient castle, an even older church, and for the peace and solitude after my visit to Pooley Bridge.

A triangular-shaped area bordered by the A66, Ullswater lake, and the A5091, is fascinating to explore. Hidden-away hamlets are sprinkled amongst the small hills and dales and linked by a bewildering maze of miniscule roads. Dacre lies in seclusion to the east of this region, about two miles from Penrith.

Dorothy Wordsworth wrote in her journal of a visit here in 1802, and the Dacre of today seems little changed. The village is an attractive collection of old cottages and farms – some very picturesque – gathered around the pub and the church.

The Parish Church and one of the Dacre Bears.

Lodge Farm.

The buildings that have not been rendered, display an unusual and beautifully coloured local stone. Iron deposits in the ground where the rock was quarried have given the harsh limestone a delicate warm pink-grey tint. Well seen in the walls of the church, the castle, and the frontage of Dalemain, a fine house about half a mile away.

This area has been inhabited for well over 1000 years, and we have the written evidence of the Venerable Bede that there was a monastery here in 698AD, probably the venue for an historic meeting in 926AD, of three kings – of England, Scotland, and Cumberland. The Scottish and Cumbrian kings did homage to the English and were baptised into Christianity.

In the 14th century there was a lot of border conflict between the Scots and the English, and the rich Cumbrian manors were being plundered by marauding Scottish raiders. A line of fortified towers were built around the Eden valley for the protection of people and stock.

Dacre Castle is a rare example of a lone pele tower that has not fallen into ruin.

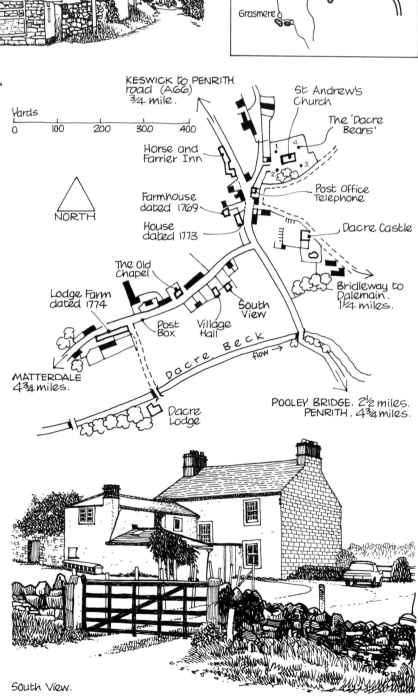

South View.

57

I parked by the pub on a steep hill. My grandad was village policeman for this area, and he could talk with feeling about having to pedal his big and heavy police bicycle over 'Dacre Banks'. It's unlikely that it was ever in hot pursuit of some master criminal astride a getaway racer.

The Horse and Farrier is a rough and ready country pub, still with the steps up the wall for mounting the last horse home after a hard night in the tap-room.

Farmhouse dated 1769.

When the Earl died in 1715, the Dacre family possessions in Cumberland were sold off. The castle was eventually bought by Edward Hassell of Dalemain and it remains part of the Hassell estate. For many years the building was neglected but now, after careful renovation it is a comfortable and extremely desirable private residence.

Horse and Farrier Inn.

Dacre Castle looks exactly like a child's toy fort. But with walls seven feet thick and 66 feet high, this most impressive edifice is no plaything, even with a pretty garden and ducks splashing in the moat.

Built for protection against Scots raiders in the 14th century, the castle ground floor housed farm stock, and people sheltered on the floors above.

Marauding was dying out by the 17th century, and the castle was made more habitable by the fifth Lord Dacre, who added the large windows.

Dacre Castle.

Terraced cottages on Matterdale road.

Four mysterious bears, carved from stone, stand at the corners of a rectangle around the church. They appear to tell a story and may have marked the extent of an earlier churchyard, but their precise significance is unknown.

The post office is hidden away in an old cottage. Over the road a cherry tree in full blossom made a wonderful show in front of an ancient farmhouse.

Across a narrow field from the castle, St Andrew's church stands on the hillside, attractively shaded by old yew trees. A beautiful building of local stone, with red sandstone battlements along the walls of the side aisles and clerestory.

This is thought to be the site of the monastery written about by Bede, but very little remains have been found. It is probable that the stone from the earlier building was used in the construction of the church, sometime during the 13th century.

The entrance is through a Norman tower and arch, into a broad nave with 500 year-old arches, and pillars 200 years older. Ancient roof beams are lit very effectively by the high clerestory windows. The oldest part of the church is the chancel – still owned by the Hasells, who have

The Post Office

The 'Dacre Bears.'

Bear sleeps...   Cat wakes bear...   Bear grabs cat...   Bear eats cat.

many family monuments around the walls. Above the altar, the east windows are quite stunning in their simplicity. A lovely parish church, and lovingly cared-for.

Dacre Beck was full beneath a pretty, stone bridge. In 1307 the beck drove the waterwheel of a fulling mill for the treatment of woollen cloth, but no trace of the mill remains.

Near the village, Dalemain has been the family home of the Hassells since 1665. The large Georgian-fronted house has magnificent gardens, and is open for public inspection and teas in the baronial hall.

The derivation of 'Dacre' is the Welsh word for 'tear', but I had felt no sadness in this peaceful village.

St Andrew's Church.

The Village Green.

Elterwater

The early Norse settlers called it, Elpt Vatn – swan lake – and now the name of Elterwater is shared by the lake and the village.

Much of the land around here used to be swamp, until it was bought up in 1820 by an enterprising man, John Harden. He deepened the lake and drained the marshes creating the landscape of bumps and hillocks we see today. In the 1830s he sold back the reclaimed land to the local farmers. At a handsome profit, no doubt.

The village of Elterwater is situated right in the entrance to Great Langdale. A position of great attraction for tourists, which has turned the village into a large and lovely, Lakeland set-piece. But, like the face of an ageing beauty changed by the cosmetician's knife, it has become almost too perfect, without blemish or character.

Elterwater is still movingly beautiful though, with magnificent surroundings that make you want to shout out in appreciation on clear days in autumn.

The road from Ambleside to Elterwater has many delights but I like to arrive over Red Bank on the back road from Grasmere. Crossing the common, which runs right into the village, there's a fabulous view over the houses to the Langdale Pikes.

Car parking in the centre of Elterwater can get a bit bad-tempered, so it's best to use the park on the common and walk. The streets are conveniently laid out for a triangular-shaped tour.

Elterwater and the Langdale Pikes.

60

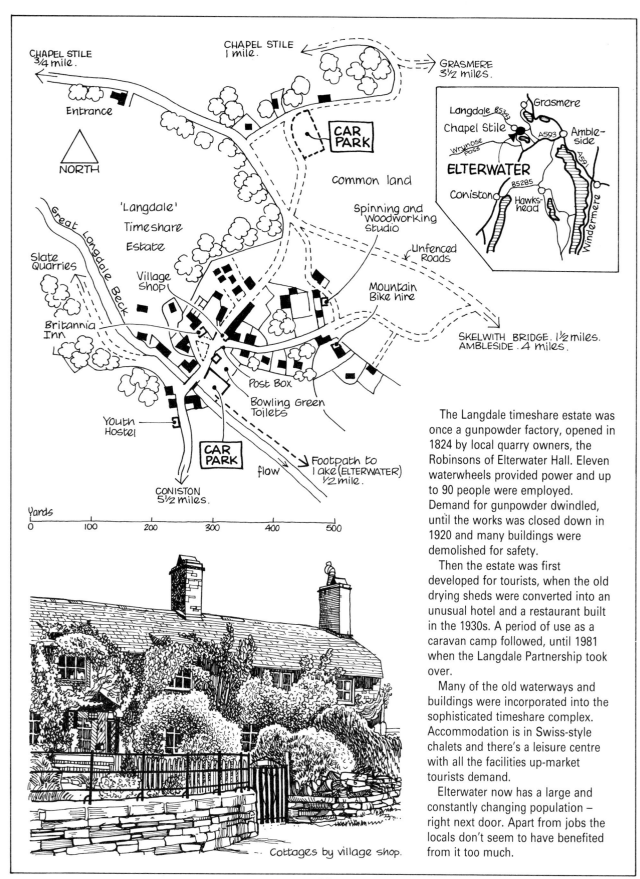

CHAPEL STILE
3/4 mile.

Entrance

CHAPEL STILE
1 mile.

GRASMERE
3½ miles.

CAR PARK

Common land

Spinning and Woodworking Studio

Unfenced Roads

NORTH

Great Langdale Beck

'Langdale'
Timeshare
Estate

Slate Quarries

Village Shop

Mountain Bike hire

Britannia Inn

SKELWITH BRIDGE. 1½ miles.
AMBLESIDE . 4 miles.

Post Box

Bowling Green
Toilets

Youth Hostel

CAR PARK

Footpath to lake (ELTERWATER) ½ mile.

flow

CONISTON
5½ miles.

Yards
0   100   200   300   400   500

Langdale B5343
Chapel Stile
Wrynose Pass
Grasmere
A593
Amble-side
ELTERWATER
A591
Coniston
B5285
Hawks-head
Windermere

Cottages by village shop.

The Langdale timeshare estate was once a gunpowder factory, opened in 1824 by local quarry owners, the Robinsons of Elterwater Hall. Eleven waterwheels provided power and up to 90 people were employed. Demand for gunpowder dwindled, until the works was closed down in 1920 and many buildings were demolished for safety.

Then the estate was first developed for tourists, when the old drying sheds were converted into an unusual hotel and a restaurant built in the 1930s. A period of use as a caravan camp followed, until 1981 when the Langdale Partnership took over.

Many of the old waterways and buildings were incorporated into the sophisticated timeshare complex. Accommodation is in Swiss-style chalets and there's a leisure centre with all the facilities up-market tourists demand.

Elterwater now has a large and constantly changing population – right next door. Apart from jobs the locals don't seem to have benefited from it too much.

61

The Britannia Inn.

As if on a pedestal, a row of slate cottages stands on a hillock, their gardens bright with colour in the sunshine. They are much photographed and make a fine picture with trees and fells in the background. One of the cottages hires out mountain bikes to madcap visitors, but nearby a lady spinning wool had found a gentler use for her wheel on a nice sunny day.

The common overlooks the village and is a grand place to picnic – sheep permitting.

A long terrace of green slate houses leads straight off the common down to the village green. Holiday flats on a grassy bank looked as though they belonged here, with unconcerned sheep grazing by the doors and piles of wooden logs outside. Lake District planning regulations make the building of new houses very difficult, so stone outhouses and sheds are often converted into living accommodation.

One perfectly-shaped sycamore tree stands in the centre of the little village green, and a picturesque 17th century pub is at the top. The Brittania Inn has low ceilings and loads of creaky character. I ate an excellent pub lunch at a table outside and purred in the warm sunshine. The bowling green across the road looked as perfect as the day.

Over the bridge, a road goes to the quarries, still being worked after 150 years, and a pleasant river-side footpath to Chapel Stile. The excellent Youth Hostel was once a 17th century farmhouse, and another – built next door in 1692 – became a centre of a linen industry started by John Ruskin of Coniston fame.

A curving road of smart houses hidden by trees, took me back onto the common.

View from Coniston road.

Holiday Flats.

62

Elterwater is a reedy, confusingly-shaped lake, quite unlike its glamorous grown-up relations with their yachts and water sports. This one is more like three tarns, where Langdale and Brathay Becks join. Considerable amounts of silt are being brought down and eventually the lake could disappear like the ancient one in Langdale. Elterwater can double in size after wet weather and has risen 5 feet in a night.

Public access is restricted to the path from the car park in the village, but the best view of the lake is from the road at the eastern end. This is one of the few lakes still in private hands. Precise ownership seems a bit unclear, but the top tarn belongs to the Langdale Partnership who keep a boat there for their employees to go fishing.

Bird life is abundant and the whooper swans who gave the lake its name are notable migrants from Siberia in the winter. As lakes go Elterwater is undramatic, but as a collection of tarns it's pretty and peaceful.

Burnhowe. Spinning and Woodturning Studio.

I returned to the village through the water meadows, looking out for the cannon which was used to test gunpowder from the factory. But it has gone, taken back inside the walls of the timeshare estate for safe keeping.

Elterwater sprang up to serve the needs of early industry, and now happily feeds the modern industry of tourism. But the ethereal beauty of the place persists so we need not weep. The swans still come and so do we.

Much photographed row of quarrymens' cottages.

The Main Street.

Eskdale Green

People who think the Lake District is over-crowded should take a ride over the Ulpha fells into Eskdale. The road rises steeply out of the Duddon Valley to a high plateau of coarse grass, from where I could see clear to Scafell without obstruction of wall, tree or house. Only sheep, who seemed larger and more unkempt than usual, inhabit this wind-blown wilderness. After that, Eskdale looked extra-lush as I sunk into the softness of the valley, awash with green and purple colour.

Direct access to Eskdale from Ravenglass is blocked by Muncaster Fell so the roads go round the obstruction, along both sides of the valley before joining up at Eskdale Green. The dale really begins at this point as the fells draw-in, growing in height and ruggedness, like an honour guard of scrummaging rugger players.

A Roman road once came through here and more recently, pack horse trails and drovers' tracks. These brought weary travellers, leading to the growth of a resting place and settlement.

The village follows a half mile of the narrow main road where it crosses the side of a steep hill. Topside is a plantation of dense conifers which overhang the houses and the road, giving the centre area a dark and oppressive atmosphere. Below the road, old houses fight for light amongst more trees. Nearer Irton Road Station the aspect is more open and pleasant. Many of the houses have 'cottage' in their names, although most are fine-looking places with plenty of garden.

FELL END

The village from Foresthow.

64

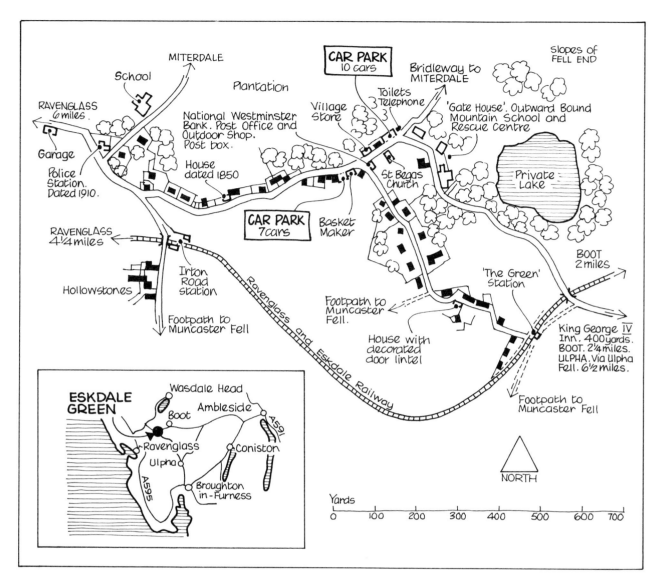

MITERDALE

School

Plantation

CAR PARK
10 cars

Bridleway to
MITERDALE

slopes of
FELL END

RAVENGLASS
6 miles.

Toilets
Telephone

Village
Store

'Gate House'. Outward Bound
Mountain School and
Rescue Centre

Garage

National Westminster
Bank. Post Office and
Outdoor Shop.
Post box.

Private
Lake

Police
Station.
Dated 1910.

House
dated 1850

St Begas
Church

CAR PARK
7 cars

Basket
Maker

BOOT
2 miles

RAVENGLASS
4¼ miles

Irton
Road
station

Ravenglass and Eskdale Railway

'The Green'
Station

Hollowstones

Footpath to
Muncaster
Fell.

King George IV
Inn. 400 yards.
BOOT. 2¼ miles.
ULPHA. Via Ulpha
Fell. 6½ miles.

Footpath to
Muncaster Fell

House with
decorated
door lintel

Footpath to
Muncaster Fell

ESKDALE
GREEN

Wasdale Head

Ambleside

A591

Boot

Ravenglass

Coniston

Ulpha

A595

Broughton
in-Furness

NORTH

Yards
0   100   200   300   400   500   600   700

Richmond Cottage.

I was very taken by Eskdale granite, used for building throughout the village. It's the most handsome of all the Lakeland rocks, with a fabulous sparkle and beautifully coloured in myriad shades of pink and blue, well displayed in the walls of the church and the police station.

There is car parking at the village centre, but few amenities to stop for, apart from the well-stocked shop. The pub is a good walk away and there's no place to eat or get a cup of tea. Farming is unobtrusive. Eskdale Green seems silently and stoically residential.

St. Begas' Church.

The Outward Bound School is located in two large country houses with extensive grounds, woods and a private lake. Residents undertake a wide range of hairy outdoor pursuits, building muscle and character. When I peeped in, two gangs of noisy youngsters were trying to push an immense football over each other. Character building, I think.

I stayed overnight just outside the village at the King George the 4th Inn. Waking up and seeing nothing out of the window but trees, fells and fields was a rare treat. The inn dates back to the 16th century with an even older cellar and the remains of a Roman bath house.

St Begas' is a modern chapel and church hall. A fine-looking building but uninspiring as a church. Next door there's a bank. Bit of a surprise this, I hadn't thought Eskdale Green to be a centre for commerce.

Underneath the bank, where the side road drops steeply, I found the delightful Post Office and outdoor shop. Closed unfortunately, but an early form of newspaper vending machine was in place outside. Operation was simple. Remove plastic bag from door knob and take out paper. Put money for paper into bag and rehang on door. How much pleasanter life is when folks can trust each other.

The Post Office.

King George IV Inn.

It was once called 'Tatty Garth' because of a nearby potato field. Also 'The King of Prussia', which had to be quickly changed when hostilities broke out with Germany. Close proximity to the Outward Bound School makes the inn a great temptation for inmates to go over the wall for a drink. The mountain rescue team at the school regularly turn-out to bring back revellers to a more spartan life style.

The old pack-horse route.

The granite bridges over the railway look terrific, like part of those pottery villages sold in barn gift shops.

A group of preservationists from Yorkshire paid for and built 'The Green' station on the railway in 1968. Surprising how intrusions from the past – some far less pretty than this – eventually become so accepted they attract dedicated admirers like these. Is it possible that the much-maligned A66 road from Penrith to Cockermouth could one day have a group of preservationists singing its praises? I rather doubt it.

Ravenglass and Eskdale Railway has a station at both ends of the village and the narrow-gauge track curves through fields to the south. At first sight it looks like a toy-town railway but the locomotives are real puffing and chuffing steam trains with grown-up drivers in peaked hats. Only the self-conscious grins and clicking cameras of the gaily-clad passengers give the game away.

Markings on the sandstone lintel of this cottage indicates the original owner was a blacksmith.

Cottage on pack-horse route.

'The Green.'

Crossing the railway at The Green brought me onto a pack-horse trail, still no more than a track underfoot. I passed some old and interesting cottages before joining a proper road which took me back to the dark plantation trees at the village centre.

Eskdale Green is an odd sort of a place, bland almost to the point of dullness, with a slightly decaying atmosphere that I hadn't noticed further up the dale at Boot. This is a peaceful resting place but now I was ready to move on.

Glenridding

Writers of glossy guide books are often a bit sniffy about Glenridding, dismissing it as no more than a car park and debarkation point for far grander sights on lake or mountain.

I've always liked to linger here. True, it can get as crowded as an international airport, but visitors are generally good-natured and happy to be in the village.

Glenridding is shut off by fells to the east and west. From the south, the road goes over Kirkstone Pass before twisting and turning its way here through Patterdale.

The road from Pooley Bridge follows the shore of Ullswater for most of the way, taking the traveller from gentle green fields to rugged mountain splendour in eight memorable miles. Glenridding stands at the head of the lake where an unremitting wall of rock – Glenridding Dodd – suddenly gives way to a narrow valley.

Car parking is plentiful and unobtrusive in the village, which is made up of two hotels, tourist shops, and rows of houses along the hillsides. Many buildings are of the local dark brown slate, so depressing-looking when wet with rain.

The head of Ullswater is blissfully beautiful and can be seen from the streets of Glenridding. Unusual this; very few Lakeland villages have lake views.

Eagle Farm.

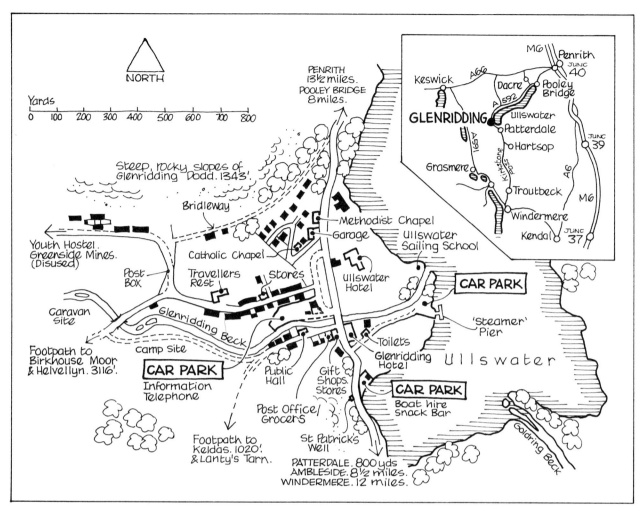

NORTH

Yards
0 100 200 300 400 500 600 700 800

PENRITH 13½ miles.
POOLEY BRIDGE 8 miles.

Steep, rocky slopes of Glenridding Dodd. 1343'.

Bridleway

Youth Hostel. Greenside Mines. (Disused)

Post BOX

Catholic Chapel

Travellers Rest

Stores

Methodist Chapel

Garage

Ullswater Sailing School

Ullswater Hotel

CAR PARK

'Steamer' Pier

Caravan site

Glenridding Beck

camp site

Footpath to Birkhouse Moor & Helvellyn. 3116'.

CAR PARK
Information Telephone

Public Hall

Gift Shops. Stores

Toilets

Glenridding Hotel

Ullswater

CAR PARK
Boat hire Snack Bar

Post Office/ Grocers

St Patrick's Well

Goldrring Beck

Footpath to Keldas. 1020'. & Lanty's Tarn.

PATTERDALE. 800 yds
AMBLESIDE. 8½ miles.
WINDERMERE. 12 miles.

M6 Penrith JUNC 40
Keswick A66 Dacre Pooley Bridge
GLENRIDDING A592 Ullswater JUNC 39
Patterdale
A591 Hartsop A6
Grasmere Kirkstone Pass M6
Troutbeck
Windermere JUNC 37
Kendal

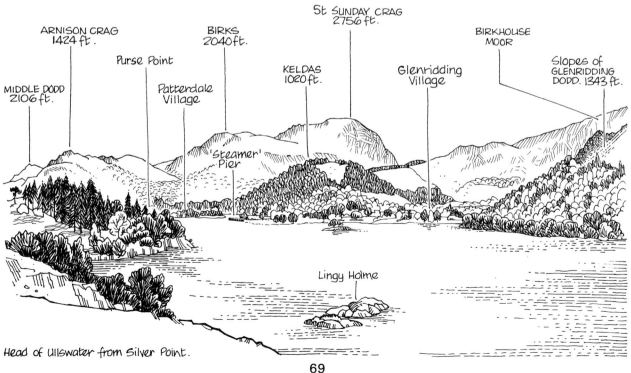

ST SUNDAY CRAG 2756 ft.

ARNISON CRAG 1424 ft.

BIRKS 2040ft.

BIRKHOUSE MOOR

Purse Point

KELDAS 1020 ft.

Glenridding Village

Slopes of GLENRIDDING DODD. 1343 ft.

MIDDLE DODD 2106 ft.

Patterdale Village

'Steamer' Pier

Lingy Holme

Head of Ullswater from Silver Point.

Methodist Chapel.

A lane goes by Eagle Farm, so ancient it appears to have sunk into the ground. Then up to the wooded crag of Keldas, prominent beside the village and a sensational viewpoint over the lake.

Glenridding Beck has been kept in check by built-up banks since disastrous floods in 1927 when a bridge was swept away and furniture was flushed out of houses across to the other side of Ullswater.

The beck has formed a delta of debris at the lakeside. A handy home for the sailing school and the landing stage of the famous Ullswater 'steamers'.

The main street has a general store and a newsagent-gift-bookshop. Both shops are friendly and unpretentious. Outside them racks of picture postcards have sheltered under a glass awning for as long as I can remember. A climbing shop round the corner makes a display of garish anoraks and blow-up boats.

The Lady of the Lake.

The road to the Travellers Rest.

'Lady of the Lake' and 'Raven' are both over 100 years old and were fitted with diesel engines long ago. They run a regular seasonal service to Pooley Bridge calling at Howtown halfway. A splendid – though often chilly – way to see the lake.

Ullswater has an unusual dog-leg shape of over seven miles long, under a mile wide and 205 feet deep in the middle reach. Rowing boats can be hired at Glenridding to explore the rocky islands and little coves and inlets. Aira Fore is a popular beauty spot and the shore nearby at Gowbarrow Park still has the wild daffodils that moved Wordsworth to write his immortal lines.

Farmers had scratched a living in this part of the valley for centuries, but the growth of Glenridding really began with the arrival of Dutch miners in the 17th century. First mining was close to the summit of Helvellyn, then in 1825 lower level workings were opened that used water power from nearby Red Tarn. Some silver was found but the Greenside mine was exceptionally rich in lead.

Huge profits were re-invested in modern machinery, production increased and Glenridding doubled in population. Reserves of ore were eventually worked out and mining ceased in 1962. The last level ran for 3000 feet into the Helvellyn mountain range. Greenside was the last and greatest of the Lake District lead mines, with a record number of years in continuous production.

I took a walk up Greenside Road between the rows of slate cottages. The steep hill brought me to the Travellers Rest, where this traveller was very happy to rest in the pleasant and peaceful pub. What a lively place it must have been when first port of call for thirsty miners just finished a shift.

Travellers' Rest.

Resuming my climb I reached a row of miners' cottages, built of the same grey slate that litters the steep fellside the dwellings cling to. Across the narrow valley, Birkhouse Moor which leads to Striding Edge and Helvellyn, loomed above me.

About the 1200 feet level spoil heaps and old mine buildings are to be found. One has been converted into a Youth Hostel.

To the right of the skyline I could pick-out the 2500 feet high, Sticks Pass where ore was carried over to the smelters at Keswick. It is amazing to see the conditions miners used to work in, and at a height only habitated these days by sheep and the orange anorak brigade.

While returning to lake-side level I paused at a high altitude post box to admire the splendid view over Glenridding and Ullswater. How welcoming it must have looked after long hours spent underground.

Back in the village, day-trippers swarmed around the sunny streets. Ice cream dripped from toddlers' fists and puffing pensioners were being hauled aboard the steamer. All of humanity seemed to be out for the day at Glenridding.

It was hard to believe that this used to be a very cut-off part of Cumbria. Then part of Stybarrow Crag was blasted away, in 1920, to make room for a proper metalled road and the great flood of motor vehicles had begun. Apart from this increasing intrusion, I never see much change at Glenridding. May it always be so.

Miners' cottages on Greenside road.

Grange

Highly-stressed urban dwellers who yearn for peace and solitude in the Lake District should not move to Grange. During a fine day in summer whole cities of people will tramp past their door. Motorists doing the round of Derwentwater will foul the air with fumes and curses.

That is the price of living at a popular beauty spot and here there is a veritable rash of them.

Grange is at the southern turning point of the road round Derwentwater, the most beautiful scenic route in the whole of the Lake District. I have seen the lake in all weathers and seasons but never been disappointed, The views, especially from the west side, are sensational.

Coming from the south over Honister Pass, the valley seems to end just after Rosthwaite in a barrier of trees and rock. However, the road twists and turns amongst oak and beech trees, crowded beneath crazy crags and cliffs. Then the road straightens out, woods clear to the left and there's Grange. Lazing in the sun – if you're lucky.

Grange Bridge and Grange Fell

Borrowdale is well-known for scenic grandeur and weather. The fact that one helped make the other is wasted on a visitor who has spent a week at Grange and never seen a mountain for mist. It does happen. Rainfall here is prodigious. Often soft and drenching, frequently in bursts of stair-rod consistency. However, rain always stops – really – and seeing Grange newly washed and cleaned, with the river a bit fuller and the fells just emerging from their misty cover, is a sight to savour for ever.

The slate-built, genteel houses of the tiny village are strung out across Borrowdale where the River Derwent widens, so the 1675 bridge needs two graceful arches to reach across. Water in the river is amazingly clear, showing off the colours of the smooth stones and pebbles to perfection.

Summer sunshine draws swarms of swimmers, canoes, blow-up dingies, picnickers, dogs and the inevitable ice-cream vans. Surprisingly, Grange takes all of it and survives, serene amongst its wild and wonderful surroundings.

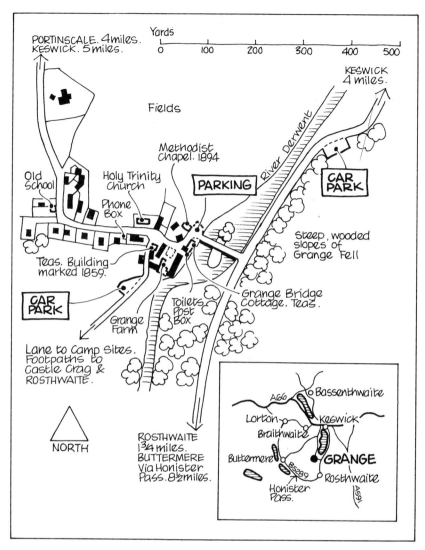

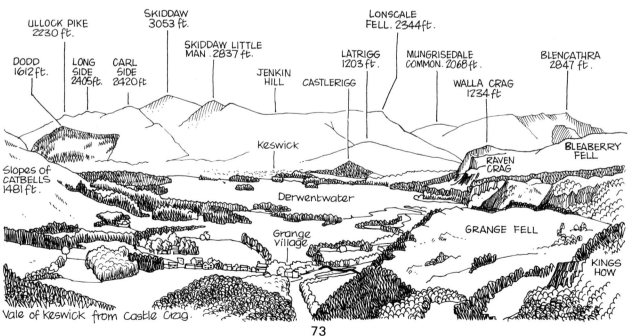

Vale of Keswick from Castle Crag.

Most of Borrowdale was owned by Furness Abbey during the 14th century and a 'grange' was built to administer local affairs. None of the settlement remains but some of the houses of modern Grange are reputed to have monastic stone in their walls.

A feature of the view of Grange Bridge is the tiny methodist church, built in 1894 to replace a Wesleyen chapel of 1859. Nearby, Holy Trinity Church is a good-looking building with a churchyard wall made of slabs of slate stuck on end in the ground. The church – built in 1860 – has a most unusual tunnel-shaped ceiling with unsettling rows of tooth-like projections.

The pair of refreshment places have tables outside where visitors can sit and get photographed by other visitors as a bit of local colour.

South of the village – like a rotten tooth in the Jaws of Borrowdale – is Castle Crag, the site of a Roman hill fort, latterly much despoiled by quarrymen. A walk to the crag from Grange is enchanting and the all-round views from the top, breathtaking. Anyone with only an afternoon to spare in Lakeland should rush here. All the drama and beauty of the district is displayed in this blessed square mile.

Central Grange

Holy Trinity Church.

CASTLE CRAG 985ft

GREAT END 2984ft

GOAT CRAG

HIGH SPY 2143ft

BLEA CRAG

MAIDEN MOOR

View to the South.

Grange Farm.

The centre of the village is laid out like a small square, probably on the plan of the monastic grange. To one side is Grange Farm, model for the house of Rogue Herries in the well-known quartet of Lakeland novels by Hugh Walpole who lived a mile away at Brackenburn.

Early tourists were fascinated by the curious 'Bowder Stone' hidden away in the woods near Grange. Today's more worldly visitors may find a huge boulder stuck on its end a bit underwhelming. It is impressive though and could weigh 2000 tons. Although the stone appears to have fallen from the cliffs of Grange Fell, experts say it was carried here from further up the valley by glacial action.

Tree planting in the 19th century has been very successful at providing an ever-changing, colourful carpet beneath the barren and broken crags around the valley.

Grange keeps her feet well out of the commercial whirlpool with just a few dignified guest houses. A discreet toilet block has recently appeared, but we should not demand too many amenities or the abundant riches Grange bestows could be destroyed.

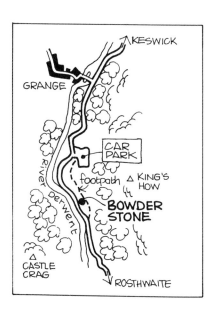

The Bowder Stone.

Grasmere

Here it is – the most famous, most visited, and most revered of all Lakeland villages. A fanfare of trumpets would not be inappropriate. People are drawn here from all over the world by the fame of William Wordsworth, but even without him, this would be a powerful tourist attraction.

Grasmere is right on the A591, main road artery through the lake district. Coming from the north through magnificent scenery, the road skirts Thirlmere before climbing over Dunmail Raise to a wide sweep down into Grasmere. Seen from this direction the summit rocks of Helm Crag take on the silhouette of the well-known 'Lion and Lamb', pointed out to passengers by generations of coach drivers.

From Windermere the traveller is taken past a kaleidoscope of picture postcard views until a sudden sharp bend reveals the much-photographed composition of Grasmere and Helm Crag.

The village and lake are cradled in a basin of low fells. Soft woods caress the slopes and embrace the meadows that melt into the water's edge. This is romantic Lakeland – gentle, refined and chocolate box pretty. Only to the north, where Seat Sandal shows its backside like a bent-over giant, does the more vulgar kind of Lakeland scenery intrude.

Shops, garage and Great Rigg.

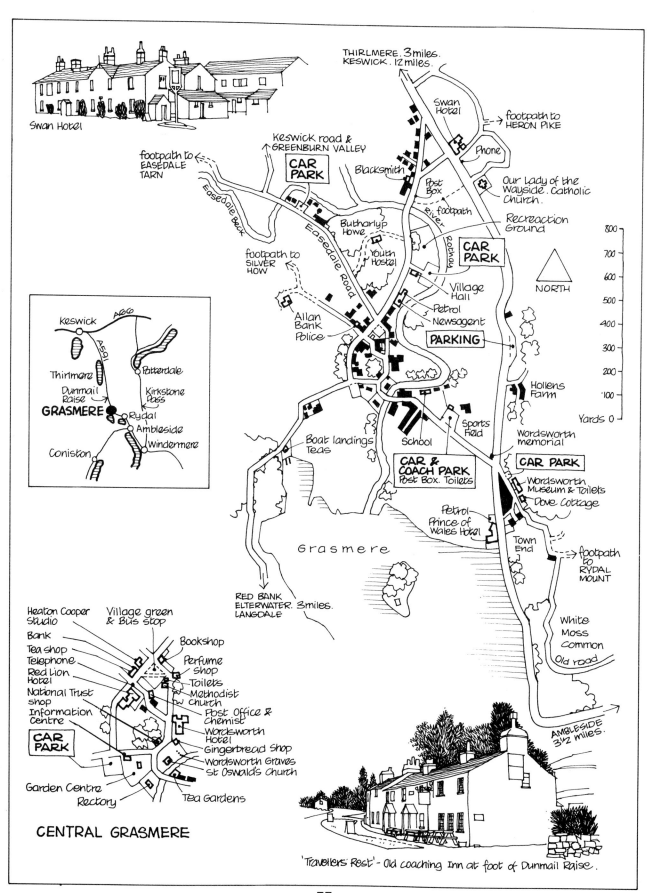

Swan Hotel

THIRLMERE. 3 miles.
KESWICK. 12 miles.

Swan Hotel

→ footpath to HERON PIKE

Phone

footpath to EASEDALE TARN

Keswick road & GREENBURN VALLEY

CAR PARK

Blacksmith

Post Box

footpath

Our Lady of the Wayside. Catholic Church.

Easedale Beck

Easedale Road

Butharlyp Howe

Youth Hostel

River Rothay

Recreation Ground

CAR PARK

Village Hall

800
700
600
500
400
300
200
100

NORTH

footpath to SILVER HOW

Allan Bank

Police

Petrol
Newsagent

PARKING

Keswick A66

A591

Thirlmere

Dunmail Raise

GRASMERE

Patterdale

Kirkstone Pass

Rydal

Ambleside

Windermere

Coniston

Hollens Farm

Yards 0

Boat landings Teas

School

Sports Field

CAR & COACH PARK
Post Box. Toilets

Wordsworth memorial

CAR PARK

Wordsworth Museum & Toilets

Dove Cottage

Petrol
Prince of Wales Hotel

Town End

footpath to RYDAL MOUNT

G r a s m e r e

RED BANK
ELTERWATER. 3 miles.
LANGDALE

White Moss Common

Old road

Heaton Cooper Studio

Village green & Bus stop

Bank

Tea shop

Telephone

Red Lion Hotel

National Trust shop

Information Centre

CAR PARK

Garden Centre

Rectory

Bookshop

Perfume shop

Toilets

Methodist church

Post Office & Chemist

Wordsworth Hotel

Gingerbread Shop

Wordsworth Graves
St Oswald's Church

Tea Gardens

AMBLESIDE 3½ miles.

CENTRAL GRASMERE

'Travellers' Rest' - Old coaching Inn at foot of Dunmail Raise.

Victorian fronted gift shops near church.

Antique shop.

Norse invaders settled in the valley during the 12th century, clearing the dense forest so they could graze their sheep. Grasmere developed a prosperous woollen industry that was almost destroyed in the 14th century when the Black Plague swept Cumbria.

After the railway was brought to Windermere in 1847, visitors began to arrive in large numbers and Grasmere was given over to tourism.

The road meanders between the buildings in a most delightful way revealing the village a little bit at a time. Grasmere has plenty of verdant trees, but they make the place seem dark and claustrophobic on wet days.

A footpath from the north end car park follows the River Rothay, low-lying and almost unseen as it twists down to the lake.

Most buildings in the central area were built in the 19th or early 20th centuries. Anything older takes a bit of finding as considerable modernisation has taken place to meet commercial pressures. Fine houses of the gentry have been turned into hotels or guest houses. The Red Lion Hotel – a small coaching inn 200 years ago – has grown to huge proportions.

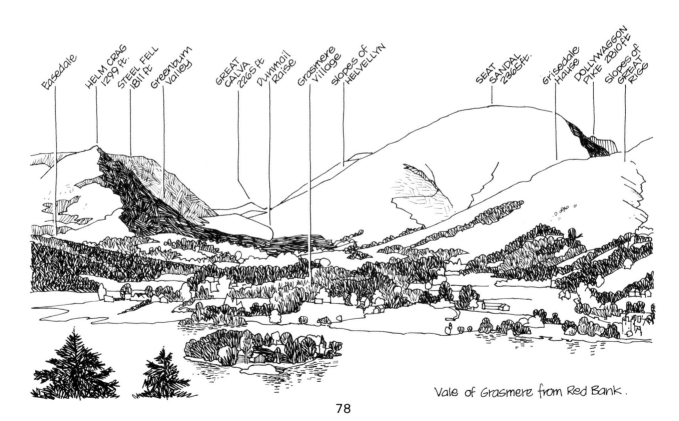

Vale of Grasmere from Red Bank.

The gleaming white Swan Hotel by the side of the main road was popular in Wordsworth's time, though not with William himself who had aversions to both strong drink and white buildings. This area of the village is mainly residential – a grey-green haze of prim slate houses.

Grasmere gift shops are admirably restrained, ranging from woollen goods and jewellery to paintings and perfume. There's even 'normal' shops – a chemist, newsagent, and supermarket.

Local artist Heaton Cooper captures all the atmosphere of the Lake District in water colours. His studio gets steamy with visitors on wet days. Sam Read's Bookshop is a splendidly chaotic place to browse among genuine Cumbria accents from behind the counter.

Grasmere Sports were started in 1868 to promote Cumberland and Westmorland style wrestling. A mysterious combative sport to the layman, where two brawny men dressed in white vests, long-johns and embroidered swimming trunks, try to break their holds on each other. Fortunately for the thousands who turn-up to watch, there are running and cycling events too, and an exciting fell race that has been run every year since 1852.

North end of village with Butharlyp How.

Rothay Bridge from churchyard.

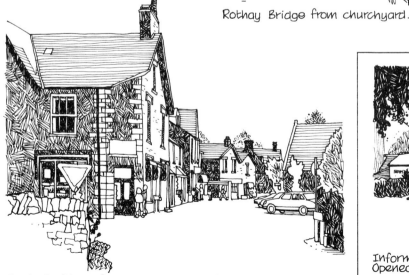

Central village from Easedale Road.

Information centre. Opened in 1986.

Dove Cottage. (1799-1808)

William Wordsworth was born at Cockermouth in 1770. After both his parents had died he was sent – aged nine – to be educated at Hawkshead. He went on to Cambridge University, then to revolutionary France where he fathered an illegitimate daughter. Returning to England, he was reunited with his sister Dorothy, to lead a nomadic life with friends before settling down together in Dove Cottage.

In 1802, William married Mary Hutchinson, a childhood friend who bore him five children. They spent a happy, if cramped, eight years here when William wrote much of his best work.

Dove Cottage is one of an inconspicuous huddle of grey houses at Town End and was once an inn on the turn-pike road from Ambleside. It's shut in now but Wordsworth had a lake view to muse over.

The small cottage and its furnishings are lovingly preserved for thousands of visitors to admire each year. Next door there is the much-praised Grasmere and Wordsworth Museum, with an old smithy converted to an excellent bookshop staffed by friendly local ladies.

Town End.

In 1808, the over-crowded Wordsworth family moved to Allan Bank, a large house below Helm Crag that William had condemned as an eyesore when it was being built. They lived here for two years with poet and sometimes friend, Coleridge. But William grew melancholic, worried about maintenance costs and the smoking chimneys, so they left – without Coleridge – for the Old Rectory in the village.

This move to a cold and damp house was not a happy one. Two of the Wordsworth children died here. Mortified, William quit the Grasmere valley in 1813, to spend the rest of his life as a country gent, two miles away at Rydal Mount. He died in 1850, Dorothy in 1855, and his wife Mary four years later. They were all buried in Grasmere churchyard.

Allan Bank is now owned by the National Trust who rent it out as a private residence. Not open to the public but very prominent in the Grasmere landscape. The Old Rectory is the home of the rector of Grasmere and still retains the Wordsworth sadness.

The Rectory (1811-1813).

Wordsworth Memorial.

William Wordsworth.
(1770-1850)

Wordsworth had a wonderfully quirky character. A small spider of a man adored all his life by two intelligent women. He was a compulsive busybody and high-minded moralist with an illegitimate daughter, often leaving his wife and children at home to go roaming the fells with his sister, and spout poetry to the sheep. The 18th century local folk thought him crazy, but since then he has fascinated millions world-wide.

Allan Bank (1808-1811) and Helm Crag.

Church interior.

The original parts of the church are the 13th century nave and tower. When the north aisle was added during the 16th century, arches were cut through the old wall. More arches were added above to support a new roof, resulting in an intricate pattern of roof timbers that is most impressive.

After the drab exterior, the brilliant white walls inside are an amazing eye-opener and with the arches, give the church interior a kind of Spanish look that is incredibly beautiful.

Until 1841, the earthen floor of the church was covered by rushes once a year. It is now flagged, but the rush-bearing ceremony is still carried-on each August.

'Rydal and Ambleside' entrance.

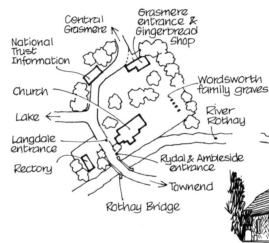

'Langdale' entrance

Grey and sombre St Oswald's was the parish church for Grasmere, Rydal and Langdale. Each township had its own separate gate to the churchyard.

The Gingerbread Shop used to be the village school-room, built in 1687, and where Wordsworth once taught. In 1854 the room was let as a home to Sarah Nelson, who first made the hard and spicy Grasmere Gingerbread that is still sold from here.

Wordsworth had a hand in most things round the village, planting the yew trees in the churchyard and even arranging the position of his own grave and the design of its headstone.

Gingerbread Shop and 'Grasmere' entrance to church yard.

The Coffee Bean. Near village green.

Red Lion Hotel.

Our Lady of the wayside. Catholic church. 1964.

Ornate cottage at Hollens Farm

National Trust information shop & Art gallery.

Heaton Cooper studio.

Quite small and shallow, Grasmere lake is unseen from the village. From the boat landings it looks devastatingly pretty, the island perfectly landscaped with trees and a barn shelter for sheep that were once boated out there to graze. Many coach trippers miss the lake, preferring to cram the gift shops instead. A pity, because this view is something most of us would like to wrap-up and take home.

Criticising Grasmere is like being unkind to a favourite Granny. Very staid and prim, determined to keep up appearances. But always reliable, always comforting. You hope she'll always be there.

Amen to that.

Boat Landings.

Hartsop

This secluded hamlet shelters between steep fellsides where Kirkstone Pass meets Brotherswater. It was once the biggest settlement and centre of industry in the Patterdale valley.

Gold and silver were found here by the Romans. In Elizabethan times lead and zinc were mined. The ore and roof slates from local quarries were carried out of the valley by pack horses along tracks still used today.

Hartsop had corn and cloth mills, with tailors, cobblers and blacksmiths looking after the needs of the miners. Houses were built around the ancient farmsteads.

Today there are no services at all. No church, no pub. The grey-blue slate buildings are laid out in a haphazard way, so the only road has to twist and turn through the village before ending-up in a good-sized car park. Nearby Pasture Beck is crossed by a pack horse bridge desecrated by ugly, wooden-fence sides.

A wide track sweeps up the valley to Hayeswater, passing a multitude of sheep pens on the way. Unusually fierce warnings to dog owners are plastered all over the gate to the fell. Sheep farming here is very big and very unprofitable. Only support from EEC subsidies and the National Trust – who own many of the farms – keep this traditional industry going. Even so, one Hartsop farm of 1700 acres has 1300 sheep.

Hartsop Dodd.

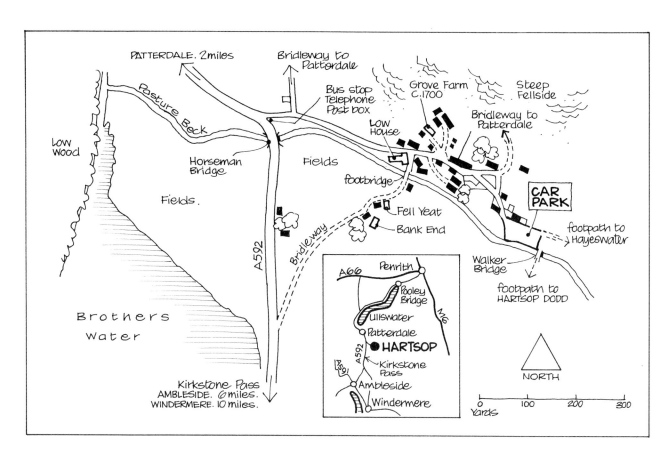

PATTERDALE. 2 miles

Bridleway to Patterdale

Grove Farm C.1700

Steep Fellside

Bus stop
Telephone
Post box

LOW
House

Bridleway to Patterdale

Posture Beck

Low
Wood

Horseman
Bridge

Fields

Fields.

footbridge

CAR PARK

Fell Yeat

Bank End

footpath to Hayeswater

A592

Bridleway

Walker Bridge

footpath to HARTSOP DODD

Brothers
Water

A66   Penrith

Pooley
Bridge

M6

Ullswater

Patterdale

A592

HARTSOP

Kirkstone
Pass

A591

Ambleside

Windermere

NORTH

Kirkstone Pass
AMBLESIDE. 6 miles.
WINDERMERE. 10 miles.

0   100   200   300
Yards

Hartsop farmhouse.

Walker Bridge
and The Knott.

The village is a marvellously chaotic jumble of tumbledown buildings, overgrown outhouses and enclosures, old gates, fences, walls and farm implements, tall trees, colourful gardens, and noisy, tail-wagging sheep dogs. Somewhere here are the remains of an 18th century corn mill and a drying kiln, but I needed an expert to point them out.

A few cottages look excessively neat, their cultivated folksiness cut-off behind high fences. Thankfully, it seems the decline of Hartsop – described by Wordsworth in his 'Guide to the Lakes', as a 'decaying hamlet' – is being halted.

Fell Yeat.

Bank End.

The oven in the wall.

I was amused by an old oven set in the wall as a place to leave bottles of milk. Some cottages have spinning galleries, probably used for passage between rooms rather than spinning. Lakeland weather is much too cold and damp to sit about outside. Fleeces were displayed on the galleries for merchants who travelled from Kendal to buy wool.

Fell Yeat was once the Bunch o' Birks Inn, on a pack horse trail that still crosses the beck at a ford before winding its way to Kirkstone Pass.

Brothers Water.

Approach from Patterdale.

The character of Brotherswater seems to vary with the weather. Usually a quiet stretch of water but often gloomy when seen from the road. A lone house is now a climbing lodge, from where lusty 'crag-rats' can look up to the objects of their desires – the crumpled rock faces at the head of Dovedale.

Low House Farm is a splendid example of a 17th century Lakeland farmstead, where a barn and cattle shed have been built on the ends of the house to help keep the humans warm.

Sheep pens and slate gateposts.

I'd used the Patterdale to Windermere road many times and never knew this tiny part of Jacobean Lake District was only half a mile away. My only regret at discovering Hartsop is that the next time I go it will not be the same exquisite surprise.

Low House farm.

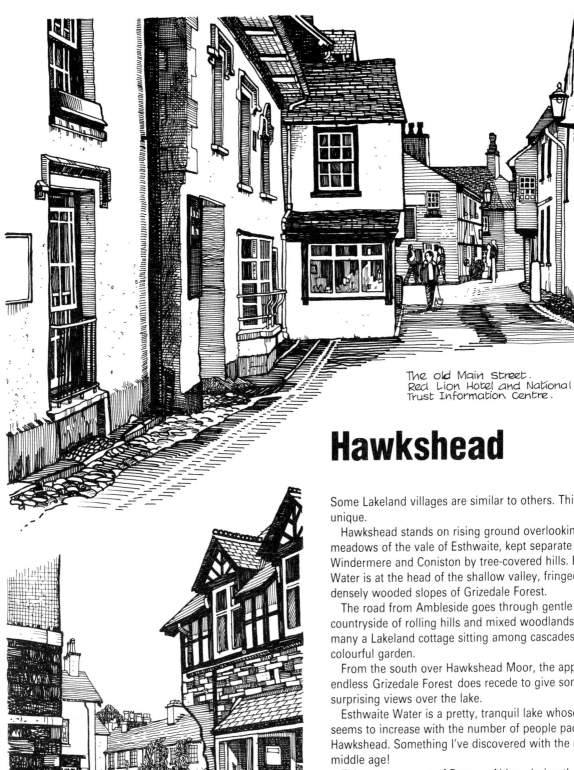

The old Main Street.
Red Lion Hotel and National
Trust Information Centre.

Hawkshead

Some Lakeland villages are similar to others. This one is unique.

Hawkshead stands on rising ground overlooking the lush meadows of the vale of Esthwaite, kept separate from Windermere and Coniston by tree-covered hills. Esthwaite Water is at the head of the shallow valley, fringed by the densely wooded slopes of Grizedale Forest.

The road from Ambleside goes through gentle countryside of rolling hills and mixed woodlands, with many a Lakeland cottage sitting among cascades of colourful garden.

From the south over Hawkshead Moor, the apparently endless Grizedale Forest does recede to give some surprising views over the lake.

Esthwaite Water is a pretty, tranquil lake whose appeal seems to increase with the number of people packing into Hawkshead. Something I've discovered with the onset of middle age!

This area was part of Furness Abbey during the 12th century. The monks built Hawkshead Hall to the north of the village and from there ran an extensive woollen business. Ruin threatened the valley when King Henry the Eighth dissolved the abbeys, but permission was given for Hawkshead to hold its own markets and fairs and it grew to be an important trading centre.

Into The Square.

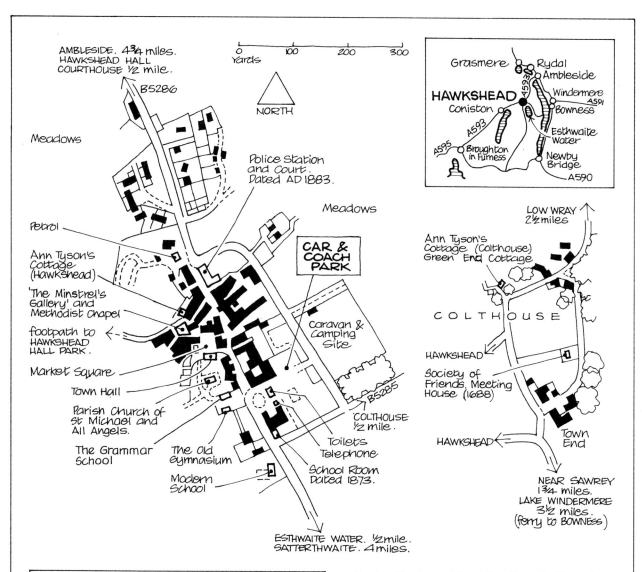

AMBLESIDE. 4¾ miles.
HAWKSHEAD HALL
COURTHOUSE ½ mile.

B5286

Meadows

Petrol

Ann Tyson's Cottage (Hawkshead)

'The Minstrel's Gallery' and Methodist Chapel

footpath to HAWKSHEAD HALL PARK.

Market Square

Town Hall

Parish Church of St Michael and All Angels.

The Grammar School

The Old Gymnasium

Modern School

Police Station and Court. Dated AD 1883.

Meadows

CAR & COACH PARK

Caravan & Camping Site

B5285

COLTHOUSE ½ mile.

Toilets Telephone

School Room Dated 1873.

ESTHWAITE WATER. ½ mile.
SATTERTHWAITE. 4 miles.

0 yards 100 200 300

NORTH

Grasmere — Rydal — Ambleside
HAWKSHEAD
Coniston — Windermere A591 — Bowness
A593 — Esthwaite Water
A595 — Broughton in Furness — Newby Bridge
A590

LOW WRAY 2½ miles

Ann Tyson's Cottage (Colthouse) Green End Cottage

COLTHOUSE

HAWKSHEAD

Society of Friends. Meeting House (1688)

HAWKSHEAD

Town End

NEAR SAWREY 1¾ miles.
LAKE WINDERMERE 3½ miles.
(ferry to BOWNESS)

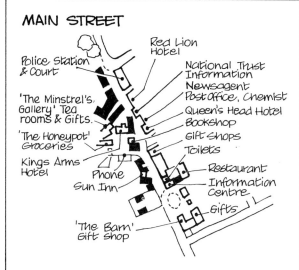

MAIN STREET

Police Station & Court

'The Minstrel's Gallery' Tea rooms & Gifts.

'The Honeypot' Groceries

Kings Arms Hotel

Phone

Sun Inn

'The Barn' Gift shop

Red Lion Hotel

National Trust Information

Newsagent Post office, Chemist

Queen's Head Hotel

Bookshop

Gift Shops

Toilets

Restaurant

Information Centre

Gifts

Road traffic, banned from the village, is directed into a sprawling car park on the outskirts. The visitor has to negotiate a whole street of gift shops before entering the village proper. So strong is the commercial pressure, I often feel that I should be paying an entrance fee.

Hawkshead is a tightly-packed cluster of old white-painted buildings separated by squares, yards, and narrow cobbled streets – many interconnected by a baffling maze of archways and alleys. There's 17th century overhung timber frames, quaint olde coaching inns, and solid slate-built Victoriana. All laid out in a gloriously disordered way, long before planning boards sat and squashed any kind of individuality.

This is paradise for students of vernacular architecture but a nightmare for makers of maps – like me.

'The Minstrel's Gallery' and Methodist Chapel.

The large police station and courtroom was built in 1883 at the north end of the village where the road diversion begins. I can remember buses squeezing their way along the main street, and I'm astonished how narrow it seems now.

One of the oldest buildings in Hawkshead is the Red Lion Hotel that was given a new front in Victorian times. Nearby is a tiny timber-framed inn – The Queen's Head – referring to that of Elizabeth the First who was on the throne when the inn was built.

At one end of the market square there is the King's Arms Hotel, with a small low-walled garden for resting the feet while exercising the arm during sunny lunchtimes. The Minstrel's Gallery, a 15th century building once the Crown and Mitre Hotel, is in a subsquare nearby. Minstrels and drinkers have long-since gone, now lunches and afternoon teas are served-up in the gracious surroundings. The Methodist Chapel looks like an ordinary house and was called the 'Unionist' Chapel for a while, so all denominations could worship here.

A lane to the left is called 'Flag Street' because of the flag stones that cover a stream still flowing beneath.

Householders used to draw water from the stream that was left open in the square. Many of the buildings here have had their corners removed to allow horse-drawn carriages to pass more easily.

Police Station and court.

King's Arms Hotel.

Before the growth of Windermere, the centre of local affairs was at Hawkshead. In 1790, much civic pride went into the building of the Town Hall that dominates the market square. Five open-arched shops known as 'The Shambles', were occupied on market days by butchers from different parts of the parish. The building was extended to commemorate Queen Victoria's Jubilee, but looks a bit redundant now. A shame for such a grand edifice.

All manner of trades were carried on in the yards and outhouses around the square. Only the grocery store and a fine modern bookshop keep any kind of commercial life going today. Cheap jewellery and dress shops have made fleeting appearances, but there were some blank, empty windows looking out on the square when I was there last. In sunshine the buildings are a blinding-white background to colourful pot plants and the pretty gardens of a row of cottages.

Main street.

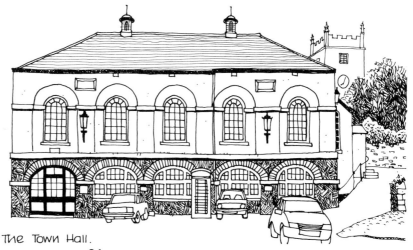

The Town Hall.

91

Parish church.

The church interior.

The parish church of St Michael and All Angels dominates the village from its magnificent hilltop situation where an ancient chapel once stood before it was replaced by the present church in the 15th century. The 'snow-white' walls, as described in verse by the schoolboy Wordsworth, have been unpoetic slate-grey since 1875, when the rendering was removed. Inside there's plenty of interest.

The Sandys Chapel was built onto the church by Edward Sandys, a locally born cleric who was made Archbishop of York by Queen Elizabeth. He was a generous benefactor to Hawkshead, founding the Grammar School by the churchyard in 1585.

Star attraction in the dusty schoolroom, where up to one hundred boys sweated over latin verbs, is the desk of William Wordsworth – encased in glass. Over the front door there's a sundial above a tablet tribute to the founder Archbishop. A row of cottages that were once the school gymnasium completes the peaceful picture.

Just down the road in lively contrast, there's a modern school of glass and bustle. While across the road, another schoolroom – of 1873 – is used by a pre-school playgroup. Nice to see the Hawkshead tradition for education is continuing.

The Grammar School.

Ann Tyson's Cottage (Hawkshead).

Ann Tyson's Cottage (Colthouse).

While a schoolboy at Hawkshead, Wordsworth lived with a local widow called Ann Tyson. For years her picturesque cottage in the village was pointed out as young William's lodging house. We now know that when Wordsworth Junior came to stay, Mrs Tyson had moved to another cottage about half a mile away in the hamlet of Colthouse. Lines in his famous poem, The Prelude, describe Esthwaite Water as seen while walking to school. A route William could only have taken from Colthouse.

Ann Tyson's cottage at Hawkshead is now rented out as a holiday home, so fans of the poet can wallow in Wordsworthian myth for a fortnight if they want.

Hawkshead plays-down the Wordsworth connection. The remarkable Grammar School seems almost forgotten amongst the glamorous woollen shops and sheep skin centres.

Hawkshead is an architectural gem that can be quite magical at times. But when the umpteenth cruiser coach draws in and the yobs stream across from the camp sites at pub opening time, I'm off – to eat my sandwiches beside Esthwaite Water.

The original Hawkshead Hall was built to the north of the village for the stewards of Furness Abbey to run their local estates. It was probably quite extensive, with barns and cattlesheds, but all that remains now is the arched gateway with the courthouse above. Rents were received here and wrong-doers tried. A gallows stood on a nearby hill.

Crudely made of rough stone, the building was restored to its present condition about a century ago. Above the archway is a sandstone niche that held a figure of the Virgin Mary until 1834.

The Old Courthouse.

Green Quarter.

Kentmere

I'd passed the signpost to it many times in Staveley, now this was to be my first expedition into the remote and mysterious valley. Hardy walkers trudge over the broad bridleway from Troutbeck, but few sightseeing motorists take the single narrow road up to Kentmere.

Beyond the pretty gardens of Staveley a skinny lake appears. It was once the site of the only deposit of diatomite mined in England, dug for industrial use by the Cape Asbestos Company. A 1000 year-old boat was dug out in 1955 before the deposits were worked out and the area reverted to its original, not unattractive, watery state.

Three miles along, the valley becomes more exposed, trees sparser and the fells wilder. A stark church and scattered farms cling to the foothills of a broken barrier of crags. More buildings spot the green hillside to the right.

Other namby-pamby villages hide themselves away, sheltering from the cruel Cumbria elements. Kentmere stands exposed, bold and defiant. Electricity only came here in 1963, piped water was a luxury in the 1940s. Even today, this is no place for wimps.

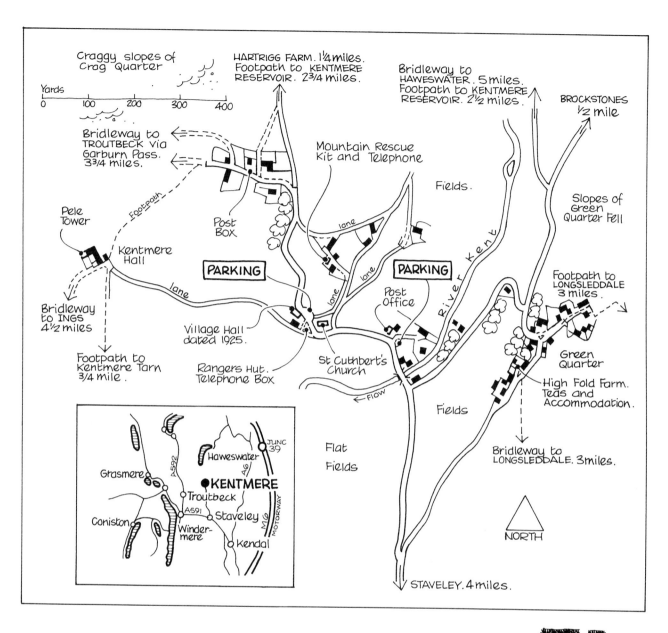

Craggy slopes of Crag Quarter

HARTRIGG FARM. 1¼ miles.
Footpath to KENTMERE
RESERVOIR. 2¾ miles.

Bridleway to
HAWESWATER. 5 miles.
Footpath to KENTMERE
RESERVOIR. 2½ miles.

BROCKSTONES
½ mile

Yards
0   100   200   300   400

Bridleway to
TROUTBECK via
Garburn Pass.
3¾ miles.

Mountain Rescue
Kit and Telephone

Fields.

Slopes of
Green
Quarter Fell

Footpath

Pele
Tower

Post
BOX

Kentmere
Hall

PARKING

PARKING

River Kent

Footpath to
LONGSLEDDALE
3 miles.

Bridleway
to INGS
4½ miles

lane

Post
Office

Green
Quarter

Footpath to
Kentmere Tarn
¾ mile.

Village Hall
dated 1925.

Rangers Hut.
Telephone Box

St Cuthbert's
Church

FLOW

Fields

High Fold Farm.
Teas and
Accommodation.

Bridleway to
LONGSLEDDALE. 3 miles.

Haweswater

JUNC
39

Grasmere

A592

A6

KENTMERE

Troutbeck

A591

Coniston

Stavely

Winder-
mere

Kendal

M6 MOTORWAY

Flat
Fields

Flat
Fields

NORTH

STAVELEY. 4 miles.

A few cars were squeezed-up by the church, the only place to park. There used to be a school, shop, pub and blacksmith here, now just a tired old wooden village hall and a hard-to-find post office are left.

Nothing at Kentmere is easy. Touring the village takes strenuous leg work. Every building is on a hill, all lanes are rough and steep. The fell terrain is so bleak and harsh, a mountain rescue centre stands always ready for use. Beef cattle and sheep have replaced the crops once grown across the flat valley floor.

MILLRIGG
KNOTT

Kentmere
Tarn.

HUGILL
FELL

View to the south.

95

Farm buildings spill down the hillsides, linked by a maze of tortuous lanes. Fields at crazy angles are littered by boulders, rocks and ancient machinery. However the modern world has made inroads. My walk through Crag Quarter was graced by a row of cottages, straight out of an estate agent's window.

I headed for Raven Crag, a huge knobble of rock prominent behind the houses. Reaching its foot, my eye was not drawn to the skyline, but to a hidden valley that was now revealed. Another two miles of farmland stretching away to the horse-shoe of fells that holds Kentmere reservoir.

The River Kent is the swiftest flowing river in the country, dropping 1000 feet in 25 miles and once provided the power for 90 mills around Kendal. To ensure a regular water flow the reservoir was built in 1848. My brief did not extend further into the wilderness, so I returned gratefully, to the church.

Bleak as its surroundings, St Cuthbert's has 16th century roofbeams but was restored in 1866 and renovated during 1950. Oil lamps with bulbs hang coldly from the ceiling. A yew tree outside is reputed to be over 500 years old and looks it.

Typical Kentmere farm.

Cottages at Crag Quarter.

Church and 500 years old Yew tree.

St. Cuthbert's Church.

A rough track leads down to Kentmere Hall, a 15th century manor house built onto an earlier, ruinous pele tower of four storeys. The interesting, though unlovely building is now a farm-house with dogs that yapped aggressively until I left.

Stone walls snake all over Kentmere, being directed in places, to include large, immovable boulders left when the valley was formed. I passed some in the road-side walls down to Low Bridge, main residential area of a few houses amongst the trees.

Farmhouse at Green Quarter.

Kentmere Hall.

RAVEN CRAG   HIGH STREET 2663ft   LINGMELL END. 2183ft   Nan Bield Pass   HARTER FELL 2539ft.   KENTMERE PIKE.2397ft

The head of Kentmere from Green Quarter.

The road to Green Quarter is steep – of course – and winds up to a well-worn green where chickens pecked between sheds grown rusty and bent. Many kinds of farm buildings jostle for positions, some in various states of lusty decay.

At High Fold Farm – crisply kept – I was served thick-sliced beef sandwiches, slabs of home-made cake and tea in a trough-sized mug. Tremendous value for money at just over a pound. The farmer's wife was preparing a caravan in the yard for visitors, now banished from the house because they used to stay in during bad weather, she said, 'using the electric'. I was pleased I'd eaten outside in the farmyard – 'softies' seem to be frowned on in these parts.

Fortified by my farm-house tea, I free-wheeled back down the hill, pausing only to puzzle over a field full of stones that looked like an ancient ruin.

Just scratching the surface of Kentmere had revealed a landscape of primitive remoteness that was faintly unsettling. But I shall return one day, physically fitter I hope, to cope with the rigours of this fascinating and lonely place.

Low Lorton

With three splendid lakes and a string of magnificent mountains, the Vale of Lorton is so richly blessed the village at its foot can seem a bit mundane.

My favourite road to Lorton is the Whinlatter Pass from Braithwaite, going through Thornthwaite Forest, now attractively landscaped to reveal some unusual views of well-known fells. Tantalising glimpses of the mountain grandeur to the south can be had from the long hill that glides down into the valley.

The village is really two – Low Lorton and High Lorton – so scattered about that neither part has an obvious centre. Cockermouth is only three miles away, close enough to have inhibited the development of many shops for either locals or visitors. There's just a couple of pubs and a post office.

Motorists are not encouraged to park in the narrow streets or use pub car parks sternly marked 'For patrons only'. I eventually found a space to park near Lorton Hall and set off to walk along the Low Lorton street. Yes, there is only one, narrow and boomerang-shaped.

Lorton Hall is well-hidden behind trees and a high wall. The gloomy, old house dated 1663, is built round a pele tower, said to be haunted by a woman holding a lighted candle.

I quickly moved on to Winder House next door, where my feet made such a noise on the gravel drive, I felt like an intruder and returned to the street.

I was pleasantly surprised by the assortment of buildings. From 17th century farm-houses and tiny cottages to modern Lakeland slate bungalows. Many of the older places have been done up to weekend cottage splendour. A gang of builders converting an outhouse were the only people I saw throughout the whole village.

House by Low Lorton bridge.

98

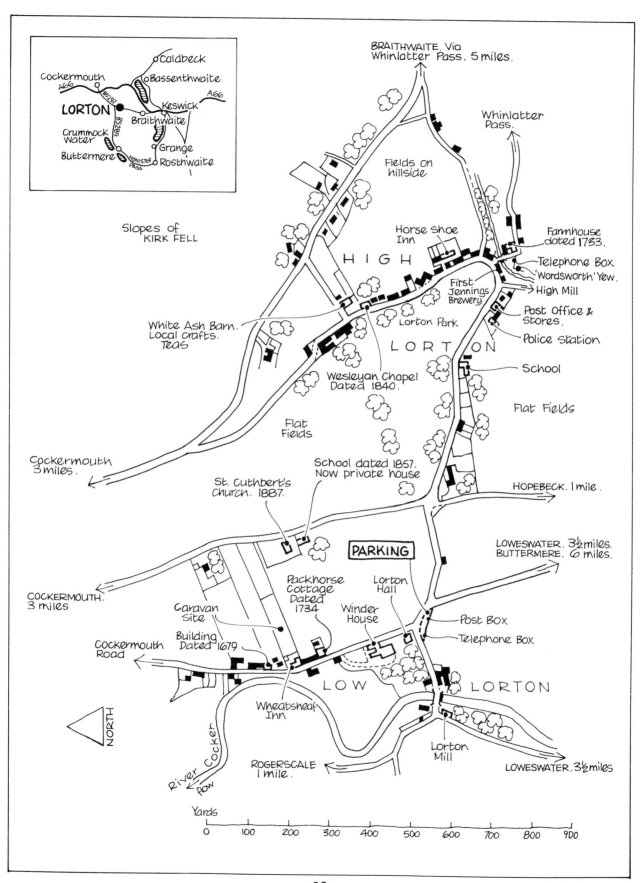

BRAITHWAITE. Via Whinlatter Pass. 5 miles.

Whinlatter Pass.

Caldbeck
Bassenthwaite
Cockermouth
A66
B5292
LORTON
B5289
Keswick
Braithwaite
A66
Crummock Water
Grange
Buttermere
MONISTER PASS
Rosthwaite

Slopes of KIRK FELL

Fields on hillside

HIGH

Horse shoe Inn

Farmhouse dated 1733.

Telephone Box
'Wordsworth' Yew.

First Jennings Brewery

High Mill

White Ash Barn. Local crafts. Teas

Lorton Park

LORTON

Post Office & Stores.

Police Station

School

Wesleyan Chapel Dated 1840.

Flat Fields

Flat Fields

Cockermouth 3 miles.

School dated 1857. Now private house

HOPEBECK. 1 mile.

St. Cuthbert's Church. 1887.

LOWESWATER. 3½ miles.
BUTTERMERE. 6 miles.

PARKING

COCKERMOUTH. 3 miles

Packhorse Cottage Dated 1734

Lorton Hall

Caravan Site

Winder House

Post Box

Telephone Box

Building Dated 1679

Cockermouth Road

LOW   LORTON

NORTH

River Cocker flow

Wheatsheaf Inn

ROGERSCALE 1 mile.

Lorton Mill

LOWESWATER. 3½ miles

Yards

0   100   200   300   400   500   600   700   800   900

The Wheatsheaf is a pleasant sparkling-white pub that sticks out into the road making this a dangerous spot for walkers. Especially when caravans are swinging into the field behind to park-up for the summer.

At this point the clear and broad River Cocker meanders up to the roadside. Do not take any of the fish. They belong to a Cockermouth fishing club, a notice points out.

Across a wide field away, I found St Cuthbert's church, pretty in icing sugar pink and blue with small lancet windows and a pinnacled tower. A large and beautiful beech tree shades the gravestone of Daniel Fisher, nobly engraved – 'On tombstones, praise is vainly spent, Good works is man's best monument'.

Next door, the old school dated 1857, has been sensitively converted to a comfortable and very impressive private house.

I returned past Lorton Hall to the graceful two-arched, stone bridge over the river. A solid-looking water mill amongst the trees is yet another old building that has been converted to rural bliss, with a manicured lawn and oil lamps in the window. Other fine houses hide behind trees, like shy country ladies not wishing to be seen.

Wheatsheaf Inn.

St. Cuthbert's Church.

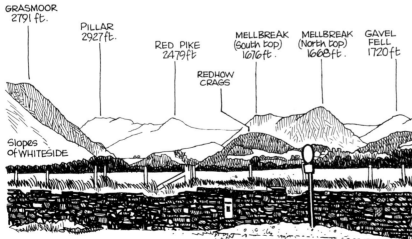

The Buttermere Valley from Low Lorton.

GRASMOOR 2791 ft.
PILLAR 2927ft.
RED PIKE 2479ft
REDHOW CRAGS
MELLBREAK (South top) 1676ft.
MELLBREAK (North top) 1668ft.
GAVEL FELL 1720ft
Slopes of WHITESIDE

Inevitably, the visitor to Low Lorton is drawn-back to temptation by the view up the valley and thoughts of that heavenly trio of lakes – Loweswater, Crummock Water, and Buttermere. I looked south, but did not linger too long. This part of the village had been so interesting I wasn't feeling too miffed about having to wander the streets of High Lorton before I could put my boots on a lake-shore.

High Lorton

Moving up to the higher village, I easily found a place to park in a wider street next to White Ash Barn, a really worthwhile barn conversion selling teas and light lunches, paintings and craft gifts.

The hill up to Whinlatter Pass is lined by big houses in large, tree-packed gardens. Trees seem to grow in abundance here, forming huge, green umbrellas over dwellings and streets, keeping off the showers – then dripping for hours.

Lorton Park is dotted by stately trees, protected from cattle by those quaint tubes of iron rails turned down at the top. The handsome house in the corner looks like a throwback to Lorton's manorial past.

Nearby, a sharp bend in the road just avoids a delicately positioned terrace of 17th century, blue and white painted cottages.

As at the lower village, my walk along the main street was in a state of pleasant surprise. Here's another picture-book gallery of houses and terraces overflowing with gardens, shrubberies and trees. All crowded and crammed together as though the valley could not spare them more space.

Some look as though they've had a bit of money spent on them. Not flashy Hollywood amounts, but a lot more than the average Cumbrian could afford. I took my time along the street, didn't rush. Not one person did I see. Was I walking a ghost-street of week-end retreats?

Farmhouse dated 1733.

Local to the tops of its smoke-blackened chimneys, the Horse Shoe Inn is hidden from the main street by a wooden bungalow. But it is worth looking for, a splendid example of an unaltered, old pack-horse inn.

At the end of the street I came to my biggest surprise. A row of ancient cottages with stone steps up to their high-placed doors, like fishermen's homes at the sea-side.

Horse Shoe Inn.

Bridge to the telephone box.

The Post Office.

The usual place to find a red telephone box is at the roadside. High Lorton has one on the grassy bank of a beck, well away from the road and near a large, scraggy yew tree.

Crossing a high stone bridge I went down to have a look at this remarkable tree. Wordsworth was so impressed with it he dashed off a poem in praise. Well, he had written about everything else. Rumour has it that during the 17th century George Fox preached Quakerism to a large crowd under this very tree.

Not being of a religious persuasion or a sensitive poet I was far more moved by the sight of the hallowed building on the other side of the beck. This was the original Jennings' brewery. Forerunner of their modern plant in Cockermouth that provides a flood of pubs throughout Cumbria with the best bitter in Britain. Local folk now use the old building as an unusual village hall.

Cottages at south end of Main Street.

After passing an impressive police station – do they really have crime here? – I came to the equally fine village school, dark and empty of pupils. Peace is one thing, but this was beginning to feel like an Alfred Hitchcock film.

Coming to the cross-roads, I decided to walk back through Low Lorton where I had last seen human life. Thankfully I found the builders were still at it. They must have thought my greeting was a bit over-cheery.

Almost-deserted Lorton had been a surprise to me, with its silent, amazing houses. Now to those lakes – certainly amazing, probably silent, but unlikely to be deserted.

Just down the road is Lorton's only shop and post office, an insecure-looking couple of grey-painted wooden buildings, closed and quiet.

Was I ever going to see anybody here?

Up Hobcarton Gill, the white rock faces below Hopegill Head showed up well beside the unfamiliar view of Grisedale Pike, so well-known as a pyramid shape in the Derwentwater skyline.

Main Street.

Terrace near Lorton Park.

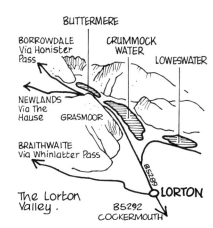

The Lorton Valley.

BUTTERMERE

BORROWDALE
Via Honister Pass

CRUMMOCK WATER

LOWESWATER

NEWLANDS
Via The Hause

GRASMOOR

BRAITHWAITE
Via Whinlatter Pass

B5289

LORTON

B5292
COCKERMOUTH

Newby Bridge

Meeting point for road, rail, and water systems, this is the Lake District equivalent of the motorway spaghetti junction. There's even a helicopter pad behind the Swan Hotel – very flash.

Newby Bridge is situated at the southern end of Windermere lake where a broad river, a rail line and the fast trunk road to Barrow-in-Furness squeeze through a bottleneck gorge of densely-wooded hills.

The bridge that gives the small cluster of hotels its name has always been an important crossing place for travellers going from one side of the lake to the other. A wooden structure that stood on stone pillars was replaced in 1652 by the present bridge. Slate-built with five, low arches carrying a narrow road with triangular-shaped laybys for pedestrians to escape the constant stream of traffic.

Windermere ends visually to the north of the village, at Lakeside, but lake jurisdiction extends down river to end at the east side of the bridge. On the west side the water officially becomes the River Leven.

A steamer service used to operate in the narrows between Lakeside and Newby Bridge using special two-bowed, paddle-boats. The stretch of water is now popular with learner canoeists.

Newby Bridge Inn.

104

Below the bridge, a concrete weir crosses the river at an acute angle retaining a head of water for emergency use; last time was in the great drought of 1984. The swirling water is overlooked by a pleasant seat from where I admired an attractive grouping of buildings across the river while eating my sandwiches.

The passing water could have fallen to earth in Grasmere or onto the Langdale Pikes. It is theoretically possible to canoe a continuous water system from Grasmere lake to Morecambe Bay, passing through Rydal Water, along the River Rothay into Windermere, down to the River Leven, Greenodd and the sea. Twenty-five miles and a long walk back to Grasmere.

Below the weir the water is very spirited, throwing itself between great boulders to the delight of white-water canoeists.

Next to the bridge itself the most conspicuous feature of Newby Bridge is the impressive-looking Swan Hotel. One of the oldest coaching inns in Cumbria, the original 1622 building has been much extended over the years to a modern luxury hotel with public restaurants and bars. A gift shop sells the usual woollen goods, country clothes and gifts.

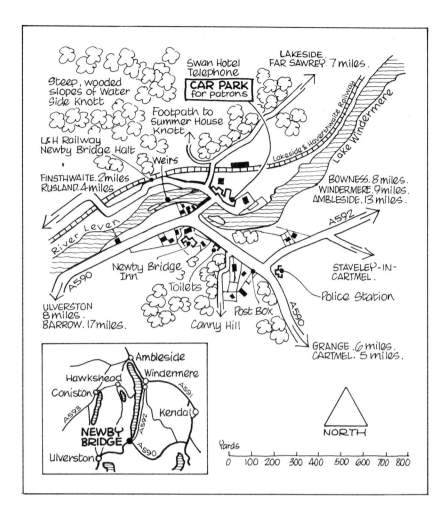

I had a drink at one of the tables beside the river while being entertained by amusing ducks and stately swans on the water. Just upstream a marina of small sailing boats bobbed in a gentle backwater making this a pleasant and gracious place to relax.

While I was looking at the helicopter pad behind the hotel a steam train suddenly thundered between the trees. Belching smoke hung in the still air. Even though the locomotives are mechanically impressive, during the steam age – en masse, they were a noisy and stinking pollutant.

The village from the south west.

A row of railwayman's cottages beside the line are still occupied. The rest of the village is made up of large houses, many of them operating as small hotels or guest houses. An old timber-framed house stands on a hill next to a large bank barn. Canny Cumbrian farmers made use of the natural hillsides by building their barns horizontally out from the slope to form a space beneath the floor, used as cattlesheds or stables. This building did not appear to be in agricultural use as the barn part had been converted into a cottage.

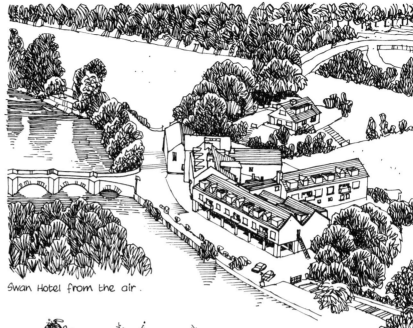

Swan Hotel from the air.

Lakeland bank barn.

With beautiful trees and a pretty – if mock – gypsy caravan in the garden, the Newby Bridge Inn looks very inviting. The hill behind the inn is covered most attractively by huge trees.

I crossed the road in some trepidation as heavy lorries charged into the sharp bend near the bridge. Compared to this wild thoroughfare, the road to Windermere looked like a quiet byway. Pennington Tower is a curious folly to be found on the wooded hillside behind the Swan Hotel.

At the turn of the century this valley was exceedingly busy. Coppice wood was cleared from the hillsides to be turned into pit props or bobbins by the local sawmills. Some wood was burnt to make charcoal for the gunpowder works, a mile downstream at Backbarrow. The large village also had an iron works and a 400 years-old mill making the famous Reckitt's Blue – first of the 'Whiter than White' washday additives. Now the building is part of the 'Lakeland Village' timeshare complex.

The Marina.

Newby Bridge Halt.

Haverthwaite

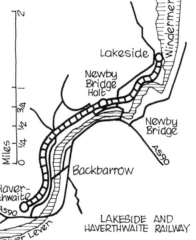

LAKESIDE AND
HAVERTHWAITE RAILWAY

Six years after British Rail closed the Ulverston to Lakeside branch line in 1967, three miles at the northern end were re-opened by a group of steam enthusiasts as the Lakeside to Haverthwaite Railway. The main station at Haverthwaite is decked out in full Victorian regalia. Trains run through woodland beside the river, stopping off at Newby Bridge before reaching Lakeside to link-up with the Windermere steamers for Ambleside or Bowness.

In the 1890s, industrial magnate H. W. Schneider used to leave his lakeside mansion, preceded by a butler carrying a laden silver tray. They boarded the private steamer 'Esperance' where Mr Schneider ate breakfast while cruising down Windermere to Lakeside, where a train awaited to convey him to the office in Barrow.

The procedure was reversed in the evenings, returning the great man back home in time to change for dinner. His house is now the Belsfield Hotel on the Bowness esplanade. After being raised from the bed of the lake in 1940 the 'Esperance' was restored and can be seen in the Windermere Steamboat Museum.

Travel today doesn't come up to the Schneider standards, but a combined trip on lake and rail can be a memorable outing.

There's only a railway platform at Newby Bridge Halt. That's the village really – nice surroundings, not too much to see, but worth hanging around in case something turns up. It is an excellent service area for all the transport systems that meet here. The petrol station is on the A590, just south of the village.

Lakeside.

Patterdale

Beginning high up on Fairfield, a rocky ridge crosses St Sunday Crag before descending to almost close off the valley where the grey, old settlement of Patterdale gathers. The village has mountain ranges on two sides so is only reached by road over Kirkstone Pass from the south or along the shores of Ullswater from the north.

Although there's a useful car park at the village centre, vehicles of fell walkers usually line the sides of Grisedale Road, beginning at the recreation field. You need to get here early in the day to get a place.

Origins of the Patterdale name are said to be founded in the visit of St Patrick during the 15th century. After being shipwrecked on the Duddon Sands he walked the thirty miles overland to this valley. Seems an odd thing to do – even for a Saint.

Slate-built houses are strung out along the through road of the village, some climbing up onto rock ledges. Walkers are a common sight, often laden down and weary after having to queue all day to cross Striding Edge to the summit of Helvellyn. In the evenings they queue for sustenance at the White Lion.

Idyllic cottage at Rooking.

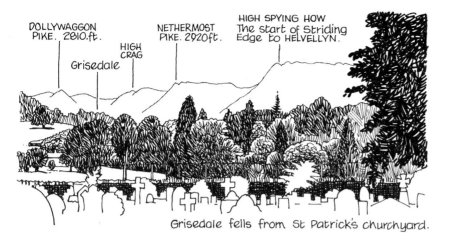

DOLLYWAGGON PIKE. 2810.ft.

HIGH CRAG

Grisedale

NETHERMOST PIKE. 2920ft.

HIGH SPYING HOW
The start of Striding Edge to HELVELLYN.

Grisedale fells from St Patrick's churchyard.

Peaceful Grisedale runs up from the village, overlooked by St Sunday Crag and Striding Edge where folk teeter excitedly on the skyline. Head of the dale is a high wall of buttressed rock only breached by Grisedale Pass, the ancient route to Grasmere.

Where the valley enters Patterdale there's a fine recreation field with tennis courts. In late summer Sheep dog Trials draw many visitors.

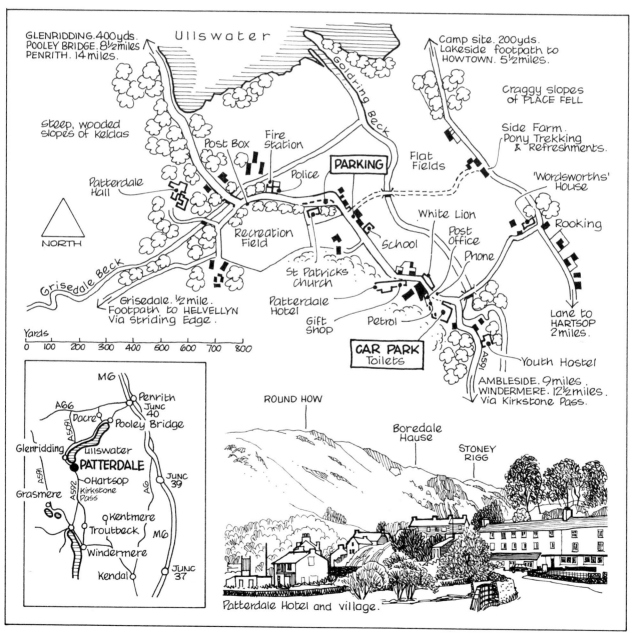

Ullswater

GLENRIDDING. 400 yds.
POOLEY BRIDGE. 8½ miles.
PENRITH. 14 miles.

Goldring Beck

Camp site. 200 yds.
Lakeside footpath to HOWTOWN. 5½ miles.

Craggy slopes of PLACE FELL

steep, wooded slopes of Keldas

Post Box

Fire Station

PARKING

Flat Fields

Side Farm.
Pony Trekking & Refreshments.

Police

'Wordsworths' House

Patterdale Hall

White Lion

Rooking

Post Office

Recreation Field

School

Phone

NORTH

St Patricks Church

Patterdale Hotel

Gift Shop

Petrol

Lane to HARTSOP 2 miles.

Grisedale Beck

Grisedale. ½ mile.
Footpath to HELVELLYN Via Striding Edge.

CAR PARK
Toilets

Youth Hostel

AMBLESIDE. 9 miles.
WINDERMERE. 12½ miles.
Via Kirkstone Pass.

Yards
0 100 200 300 400 500 600 700 800

M6

Penrith
JUNC 40

A66

Dacre

Pooley Bridge

Glenridding

Ullswater

PATTERDALE

JUNC 39

Grasmere

Hartsop
Kirkstone Pass

Kentmere

Troutbeck

M6

Windermere

Kendal

JUNC 37

ROUND HOW

Boredale Hause

STONEY RIGG

Patterdale Hotel and village.

109

White Lion.

I've always been fond of the huddle of buildings at the centre of Patterdale, now almost a Lakeland icon with the distinctive shape of the White Lion tapering like the bows of a ship towards the south. There is no apparent reason for this curiosity, the adjoining field looks as though it could easily have accommodated a conventional square-shaped building.

The post office and gift shop are comfortably old-fashioned. Picture postcards in the windows have had their bright colours bleached out by years of sunshine. Across a twin-arched stone bridge a lane goes over the valley to some blissful cottages at Rooking.

When visiting Patterdale, William and Dorothy Wordsworth stayed with their friends, Captain and Mrs Luff at Side Farm – now a popular base for pony trekking and little changed.

Carrying on a family tradition Dorothy Wordsworth complained about the colour of Patterdale Hall when it was built in 1796. The colour was changed. Today's hall has been much extended and is a YMCA outdoor activity centre.

Wordsworth Cottage stands on land that was bought by Lord Lowther in 1806 as a gift for William Wordsworth. The poet thought the price Lowther had paid was too high and went into an artistic sulk. He abandoned plans to build on the site, selling it to the local inn-keeper in 1834.

White-painted Patterdale Hotel is a large, grand-looking establishment that seems a bit at odds with the rest of the simple, slate-built village. Down the road there's a school, a police station and a fire station. A reminder that though often crowded, Patterdale is quite remote when it comes to getting a fire engine to an emergency.

The Gift Shop.

110

St. Patrick's Church.

When the Lake District began to grow in popularity with Victorian tourists, a medieval chapel at Patterdale was replaced in 1853 by St Patrick's church. A lovely, local slate-built building with a bell tower spoiled by a badly-placed clock, but still full of interest for the visitor.

The font dates from 1200 and comes from the original chapel. A white ensign that was flown during the battle of Jutland hangs from the high ceiling.

St Patrick's Well.

Wordsworth Cottage.

Glenridding silver was used to make a valuable cup in the church and lead from the same mine went into the window sills. Remarkable tapestries on the walls are the work of Ann Macbeth who died in 1948 after living in Patterdale for most of her life. She had many homes around the valley, including Wordsworth Cottage and another high up on the rocks above Hartsop.

Patterdale has a rugged, much-loved charm and is much more of a real village than near-neighbour, Glenridding. But it is the mountains that draw the big crowds, to erode the footpaths and demand more facilities.

Thankfully, diminution of the fells and modernisation of the village seems to move at about the same rate so both should see out my time – and yours – without changing too much.

Side Farm.

111

Pooley Bridge

I lived in this village until I was ten years old, so what follows could be a serious outbreak of melancholic nostalgia. Readers who dislike such indulgence should just look at the pictures or move on to Ravenglass.

The road to Pooley Bridge leaves a maze of motorways at Penrith to plunge into gentle countryside dotted by ancient remains and historic buildings, arriving on the brow of a hill that looks over the village, Ullswater and distant fells.

Coming from Glenridding the road is memorable, but a trip down Ullswater is the best way to see the remarkable change in landscape between head and foot. Pooley Bridge can easily be explored between steamer stops.

The village is small and compact with plain, rendered buildings like the back streets of an old town. Pooley Bridge was once part of the huge, medieval parish of Barton. The village square was used for sheep, cattle and fish markets.

As the River Eamont leaves Ullswater it is crossed by a narrow, three-arched bridge, an ancient crossing place and more recently the border between Cumberland and Westmorland.

Car parking is plentiful in and around the square, with another park at the foot of the wonderfully wooded hill of Dunmallet – getting a bit thin on top now. I remember snowdrops, primroses, and bluebells growing in abundance between the trees. My favourite cherry tree of forty years ago is still there.

The old smithy.

The Square.

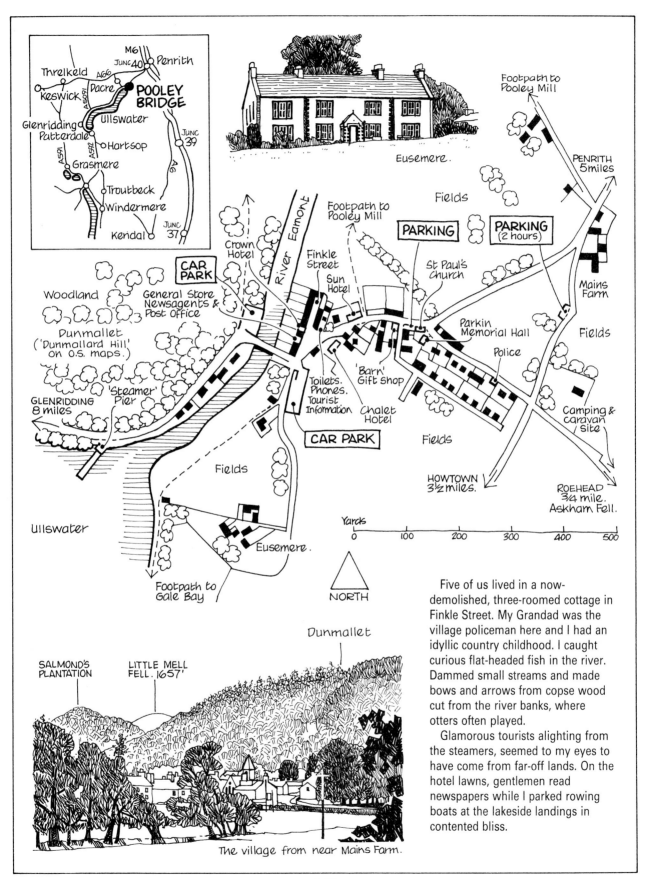

MAP LABELS:

POOLEY BRIDGE

M6 — Junc 40 — Penrith
Threlkeld — A66 — Pacre
Keswick
Ullswater
Glenridding — Patterdale
Junc 39
Hartsop
Grasmere
Troutbeck
Windermere
Kendal — Junc 37

Eusemere.

Footpath to Pooley Mill

Fields

PARKING
PARKING (2 hours)

PENRITH 5 miles

Mains Farm

Fields

St Paul's Church

River Eamont

Crown Hotel

CAR PARK

Footpath to Pooley Mill

Finkle Street

Sun Hotel

General Store Newsagents & Post Office

Woodland

Dunmallet ('Dunmallard Hill' on O.S. maps.)

Parkin Memorial Hall

Police

'Steamer' Pier

GLENRIDDING 8 miles

Toilets. Phones. Tourist Information

'Barn' Gift Shop

Chalet Hotel

CAR PARK

Fields

Camping & caravan site

Fields

HOWTOWN 3½ miles.

ROEHEAD ¾ mile. Askham Fell.

Ullswater

Fields

Eusemere.

Footpath to Gale Bay

Yards
0 100 200 300 400 500

NORTH

SALMOND'S PLANTATION

LITTLE MELL FELL. 1657'

Dunmallet

The village from near Mains Farm.

Five of us lived in a now-demolished, three-roomed cottage in Finkle Street. My Grandad was the village policeman here and I had an idyllic country childhood. I caught curious flat-headed fish in the river. Dammed small streams and made bows and arrows from copse wood cut from the river banks, where otters often played.

Glamorous tourists alighting from the steamers, seemed to my eyes to have come from far-off lands. On the hotel lawns, gentlemen read newspapers while I parked rowing boats at the lakeside landings in contented bliss.

Pretty cottages and an old smithy at the east end of the village seem little changed. The Parkin Memorial Hall is Victorian stern as ever, next to high-roofed St Paul's Church, built in 1868 with a characteristic bell tower and spire. Coulsen's farm is completely gone, replaced by a pleasant estate of green slate bungalows and a Barn Gift Shop. Not the usual pot-pourri place, this one has a bit of individuality with gifts of local interest.

The old Sun Hotel is just hanging on to its gentility. A sad note pinned to the battered front door says it all – 'No leathers or helmets'.

Finkle Street.

St. Paul's church.

Dead-end Finkle Street, my lively childhood playground, is silent now, old cottages sad-faced in modern kitsch of porches, potted plants, piles of stones and carriage lamps. Part-time country idylls with intruder alarms.

Once a blaze of sunny yellow at the top of the street, the Crown Hotel is now resplendent in battleship-grey. Elegant as a heap of cement blocks. The Chalet Hotel across the road has been cruelly shorn of all dignified shrubberies and lawns to make way for a beer garden of monumental ugliness.

River-side gardens seen from the bridge.

Chalet Hotel.

The Ullswater steamers were a much-loved feature of my early years. Captain Band was a neighbour of ours in Finkle Street who used to give me free trips, as romantic to a small boy as crossing the Atlantic. Ullswater is wide and open in the lower reach, giving good sailing for the yachts bobbing in Eusemere Bay.

Although Pooley Bridge is popular with today's tourists, I had found the village sadly changed. But childhood memories rarely are the best of witnesses.

Cafés and gift shops around the square are ghastly. Two bright spots amongst the dross are a new information centre and the general store, bright and cheerful as a camp-site shop. Considering the number of tents and caravans in this area, I suppose that's what it is.

The old stone bridge felt like an old friend as I leant over the wall to find the river of my childhood gone. Dredged and deepened to a fast-flowing sterile flood, the River Eamont of today tops-up Haweswater reservoir through an underground pumping station near the village. It could have been much worse.

Ash trees by the river have been felled to give a good view up the lake to Hallin Fell. Hiding behind a high wall on a hill is Eusemere, once the home of Thomas Clarkson, a notable campaigner against slavery until it was abolished in 1802. Dorothy and William Wordsworth stayed here for a month complaining that they couldn't see the lake for the trees. Oh dear, there's always something.

After passing some extravagant Dallas-style bungalows along the riverbank I came to the steamer pier.

Crown Hotel and Finkle Street.

'Steamer' Pier.

Pooley Bridge.

115

Ravenglass

Not all of Cumbria is lakes and mountains, some of it comes down to paddle at the seaside. Ravenglass is situated in the estuary of three rivers – the Irt, the Mite and the Esk. It's a natural harbour, sheltered from the Irish Sea by a broad expanse of sand flats, dunes and mud. The Romans made this the naval base for the whole of their occupation of north-west England, building a large fort on the shore.

Rather remote from the rest of the Lake District, the village can be reached by crossing Hardknott and Wrynose passes then driving down the narrow road through Eskdale. Not the best way to see the valley.

An even longer drive is on the A595, main West Cumbria highway. Quite interesting coming from the north, passing industrial areas and the controversial Sellafield nuclear plant. More rural from the south with some good fell and sea views.

Ravenglass is just off the main road, without through traffic. The single street follows an outcrop of land before ending abruptly on the rocky shore. Oldest houses are on the seaward side, appearing to be carved out of the very rock they stand on.

In 1208 the village was given a market charter, a cross was erected in the main street and fairs were held until around 1800.

The village and beach.

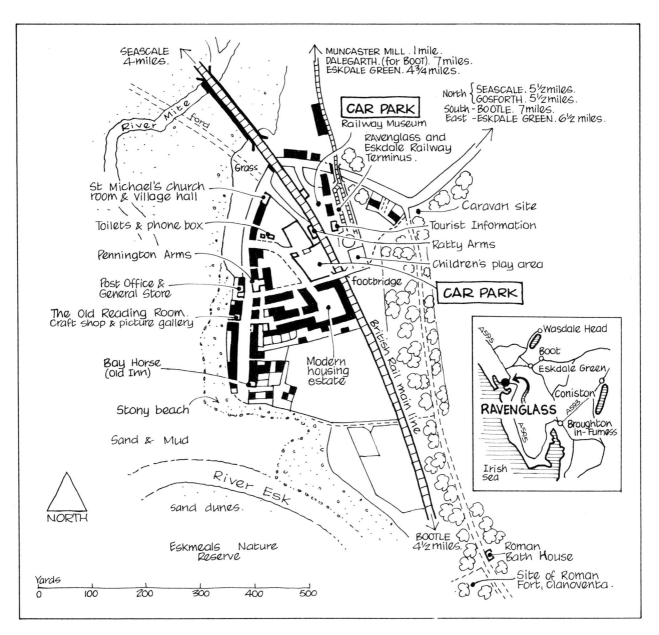

SEASCALE
4-miles.

MUNCASTER MILL . 1 mile .
DALEGARTH . (for BOOT) . 7 miles .
ESKDALE GREEN . 4¾ miles .

North { SEASCALE . 5½ miles .
       { GOSFORTH . 5½ miles .
South - BOOTLE . 7 miles .
East - ESKDALE GREEN . 6½ miles .

River Mite   ford

Grass

CAR PARK
Railway Museum

RAVENGLASS and
Eskdale Railway
Terminus .

St Michael's church
room & village hall

Toilets & phone box

Pennington Arms

Post Office &
General Store

The Old Reading Room.
Craft shop & picture gallery

Bay Horse
(Old Inn)

Stony beach

Sand & Mud

Caravan site

Tourist Information

Ratty Arms

Children's play area

footbridge

CAR PARK

Modern
housing
estate

British Rail main line

Wasdale Head
A595
Boot
Eskdale Green
Coniston
RAVENGLASS
A595
Broughton
in-Furness
A595
Irish
sea

River Esk

sand dunes.

NORTH

Eskmeals Nature
Reserve

BOOTLE
4½ miles.

Roman
Bath House

Site of Roman
Fort, Clanoventa .

Yards
0   100   200   300   400   500

South end of village and beach.

117

Post Office and Pennington Arms.

Bay Horse.

St. Michael's church room & village hall.

National television and press advertising now brings many people to see the pro-nuclear exhibition at Sellafield. After that there is nowhere else to go but Ravenglass, which has led to a stirring of change in the village over the last few years. A large car park has been opened, a modern housing estate built, and new money has come in to buy cottages as week-end sailing retreats.

In the car park, I found local ladies cleaning luxury coaches while their passengers were being shown Eskdale from the comfort of the miniature railway. Package tour efficiency has arrived at Ravenglass.

A familiar seaside smell drew me to a fish and chip shop, the first one I'd seen in any of the villages. Across the road there's an open stretch of grass where a row of cottages once stood looking over the beach and an ugly, steel bridge that carries the main railway line across the estuary.

"La'al Ratty" at Muncaster Mill.

A bottleneck is formed in the road by the Pennington Arms and the Post Office, then it opens out to a wide street, bleached by sea spray and devoid of trees or vegetation.

The short walk down to the seashore is lined by a great variety of buildings. Old farm-houses and inns, terraced cottages, an ancient shop selling paintings and sea curios, and a tumble-down garage with 1950s' petrol pumps. Stacks of building materials stood around when I was last there, so things may have changed by now.

Two tiny, 17th century cottages house the Post Office, while across the road, The Pennington Arms – a good, old sea-front inn – offers accommodation and meals.

I went through a storm gate that bristles with rubber seals to keep out the high tides, onto the stony beach, strung with breezy clothes lines. The houses grow straight out of the rocks like a cliff face. Rickety ladders lead down to the shore from small yards and doorways as if from American Indian cliff dwellings. Small boats gently bobbed at anchor in the grey water.

Across the sand dunes to the north there is the Ravenglass Nature Reserve, packed with rare plants, animals and birds. Many thousands of gulls happily paddle about in the mud; radio-active to dangerous levels, some say. To the south, Eskmeals Nature Reserve provides similar attractions for birdwatchers, naturalists and anti-nuclear protesters.

The beach.

119

Star attraction in the village is the Ravenglass and Eskdale Railway, affectionately known as 'La'al Ratty'. The station is a fascinating place with engine sheds, a turntable, signals and proper platforms that are sheltered by the familiar BR station awnings.

First opened as a three foot gauge in 1875, the line carried iron ore from the mines, seven miles away in Eskdale. Passengers were first carried a year later, before troubled times arrived.

Ravenglass Station.

"La'al Ratty".

Although both the railway and mining companies went bust, the line struggled on until 1913 when it had to be dismantled. Two years later it was re-opened with fifteen inch gauge steam trains to carry goods, passengers and mail. After the war a decline set in, ending in 1960 when the railway was bought at auction by a preservation society helped by a public appeal for money.

The Railway Museum tells the history of the now world-famous line, still run mainly by volunteers.

120

Muncaster Mill.

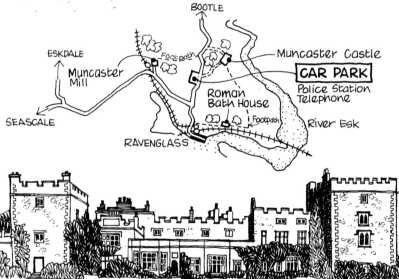

Muncaster Castle.

Trains stop just outside the village at the 18th century Muncaster Mill, a restored water-powered corn mill that sells freshly-milled flour products to visitors.

Home of the Pennington family since the 13th century, Muncaster Castle is renowned for its art treasures and fabulous rhododendron garden. A large heronry and an exotic bird garden are among other attractions.

Little remains of the Roman fort that held 1000 men, thought to have been situated in woods adjoining the village. However, the fort bath house, known as Walls Castle, can be seen – the highest standing remains of a Roman building in this country.

The results of Man's passage through history can be traced all around this most unusual and interesting village. From Roman and Viking sea invasions through trading and industrial decline, to the nuclear age, tourism, and weekend sailors' cottages.

I hope that it doesn't become too much of a tarted-up set piece; Ravenglass will do for me just as it is.

The Roman Bath House.

121

The village and Knotts.

Rosthwaite

Planning mistakes in the Lake District are all too obvious. When an eye-sore of a building blights the landscape or a new road cuts a wide swath through ancient meadows we complain loudly, enquiring what are these planners doing? Most of the time, they are protecting villages like Rosthwaite.

Borrowdale attracts many thousands of visitors, representing huge profits for any developer who could get a foothold in the valley. There is very little recent building here so lots of applications to build must get turned down. This is positive planning action, unpraised and generally unseen by most of us. Without such acts, places like Rosthwaite would look very different; pretty villages do not stay pretty by chance these days. Planners stop us destroying the very things we want to see. They should be praised.

Motorists take the spectacular scenic route here from Keswick or the equally sensational way over Honister Pass from Buttermere.

Rosthwaite is surrounded by craggy and colourful fells, mantled on their lower slopes by attractive trees. The village stands at the centre of the flat valley floor, between two rivers and sheltered by a rocky hill crowned by trees. A wonderful setting.

There are two car parks that fill up very quickly on fine days.

Yew Tree Farm.

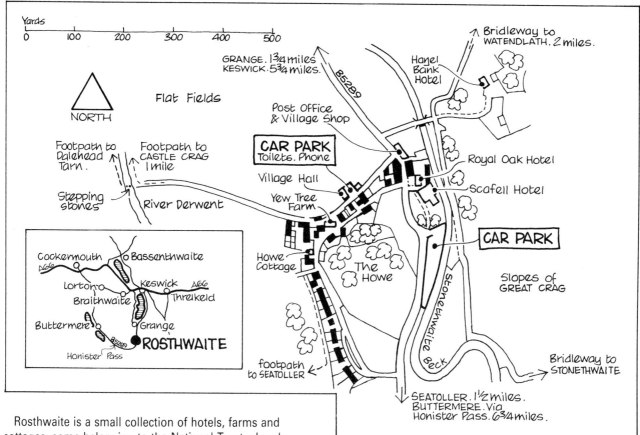

Yards

0   100   200   300   400   500

NORTH

Flat Fields

GRANGE. 1¾ miles
KESWICK. 5¾ miles.

B5289

Bridleway to WATENDLATH. 2 miles.

Hazel Bank Hotel

Post Office & Village Shop

Footpath to Dalehead Tarn.

Footpath to CASTLE CRAG 1 mile

Stepping stones

River Derwent

CAR PARK Toilets. Phone

Village Hall

Yew Tree Farm

Royal Oak Hotel

Scafell Hotel

CAR PARK

Howe Cottage

The Howe

Slopes of GREAT CRAG

Cockermouth A66 o Bassenthwaite
Lorton o o Keswick A66
Braithwaite o Threlkeld
Buttermere o o Grange
ROSTHWAITE
Honister Pass B5289

Stonethwaite Beck

footpath to SEATOLLER

Bridleway to STONETHWAITE

SEATOLLER. 1½ miles.
BUTTERMERE. Via Honister Pass. 6¾ miles.

Rosthwaite is a small collection of hotels, farms and cottages, some belonging to the National Trust who also own most of the broadleaf woodland on the fellsides. Motorists see the village only as a narrow bottleneck, because most of the buildings lie off the road down towards the River Derwent.

Rain in Borrowdale is legendary. Seathwaite at the head of the vale is the wettest inhabited place in England with 130 inches a year. Thankfully, that amount is not general throughout the area, five miles away at Keswick the figure dramatically falls to about 50 inches a year.

With two gluttonous rivers, Rosthwaite is prone to floods, so the motorist should not ignore the marked posts indicating the depth of water lying across the road.

A new car park with toilets has recently opened next to the village hall. I prefer the park next to Stonethwaite Beck where you can have a look at the remarkable banks of smooth stones, polished by the violent action of the river. The two main hotels are pleasant country establishments with restaurants and bars for non-residents.

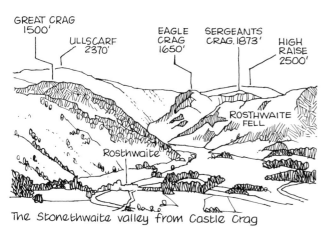

GREAT CRAG 1500'
ULLSCARF 2370'
EAGLE CRAG 1650'
SERGEANTS CRAG. 1873'
HIGH RAISE 2500'
ROSTHWAITE FELL
Rosthwaite

The Stonethwaite valley from Castle Crag

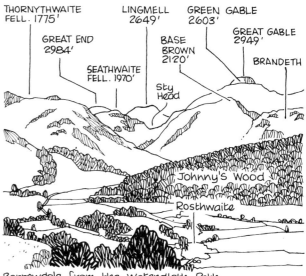

THORNYTHWAITE FELL. 1775'
GREAT END 2984'
SEATHWAITE FELL. 1970'
LINGMELL 2649'
BASE BROWN 2120'
Sty Head
GREEN GABLE 2603'
GREAT GABLE 2949'
BRANDETH
Johnny's Wood
Rosthwaite

Borrowdale from the Watendlath Path.

Howe Cottage.

The River Derwent runs wide and shallow here, an old pack horse ford has stepping stones set among the twinkling ripples. Just downstream there's a new stone bridge, built in authentic pack horse style. It's wonderful to see how much care is taken not to spoil this magnificent valley.

I returned up the lane reflecting that the first time I saw Rosthwaite was when I camped here during a journey for my first class Boy Scout badge.

Cottages in the road bottleneck look old and grey, with the passage of many motor vehicles showing on their grimy faces. Across the road, the post office is a colourful contrast with variegated ivy and pretty little blinds over the windows. Inside the slate-built shop there's everything from ice-cream to potatoes on sale.

High stone walls and farm buildings line the lane down to the river, Yew Tree Farm is especially pleasing.

The Post Office.

Some modern youths, far more adventurous and affluent than I ever was, were tinkering with their high-powered motor bikes in a barn workshop. Bus services for villages have almost disappeared and local youngsters need their own transport to get them to the towns and often, to school.

I passed Howe Cottage and some modern bungalows before arriving at a row of slate-built council houses perfectly in tune with their surroundings. Why can't other villages have good-looking council properties like these, instead of the concrete or brick-built monstrosities we see up and down the country?

Royal Oak Hotel.

Castle Crag.

Hazel Bank Hotel.

From Rosthwaite there's some great views of Castle Crag, much prettier looking than from the Grange side. Behind it, the broken cliffs of Low Scawdel are a tremendous sight.

On my way back to the main road I passed many pretty little corners before I crossed the bridge onto the Watendlath path. This ancient pack horse track, now wide and worn on the higher reaches, is the path to Mecca for many booted pilgrims. I shall return to sing the praises of Watendlath, now I wanted to have a look at the Hazel Bank Hotel. This was the setting that Hugh Walpole chose for the house of his hero in the Rogue Herries saga of books. It's a bit undramatic without the Walpole prose but a grand setting nevertheless.

Everywhere in Borrowdale has wonderful surroundings. Although the weather can be as horrible as the crowds, this valley has everything for me. Magnificent mountains at its head, a lovely and romantic lake at its foot. All of Man's needs for physical challenge, beauty and spiritual peace can be satisfied here. Rosthwaite fits in perfectly.

Eagle Crag and Council Houses.

Scafell Hotel.

125

Rydal

Holiday traffic pours through Rydal like sand in an egg timer. A spur of Loughrigg Fell creates a bottleneck between Rydal Water and Ambleside that both the main A593 road and the River Rothay have to squeeze through.

The finest way to approach Rydal is on foot. An easy fellside track from Grasmere gives superb views over Rydal Water. From Ambleside, the path through Rydal Park is a grand walk. (See Walk 3).

Rydal is a select hamlet of fine houses and cottages spread thinly round the junction of the A591 and the lane that leads up the hill to the big star residence – Rydal Mount, home of William Wordsworth until his death in 1850. There's a car park for visitors to the Mount, other motorists cram their vehicles nose to tail, up the steep laneside.

The River Rothay is crossed by Pelter Bridge, the attractive entrance to Rydal Park where Dr Arnold of Rugby School once had a house. Wordsworth used to drop round to advise him on education.

Church Cottage.

Pelter Bridge.

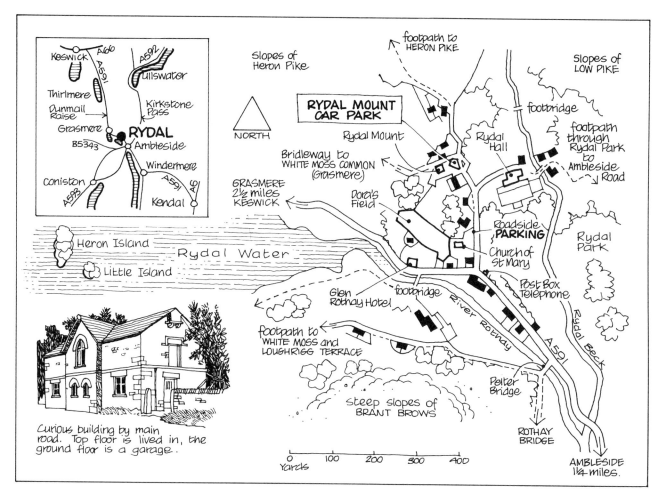

RYDAL

Inset map:
Keswick — A66
A591
A592 — Ullswater
Thirlmere
Kirkstone Pass
Dunmail Raise
Grasmere
B5343
RYDAL
Ambleside
Windermere
Coniston
A593
A591
A591
A592
Kendal

NORTH

RYDAL MOUNT CAR PARK

Slopes of Heron Pike

footpath to HERON PIKE

Slopes of LOW PIKE

footbridge

Rydal Mount

Rydal Hall

footpath through Rydal Park to Ambleside Road

Bridleway to WHITE MOSS COMMON (Grasmere)

Dora's Field

Roadside **PARKING**

Rydal Park

GRASMERE 2½ miles KESWICK

Church of St Mary

Heron Island

Little Island

Rydal Water

Post Box Telephone

Rydal Beck

Glen Rothay Hotel

footbridge

River Rothay

A591

footpath to WHITE MOSS and LOUGHRIGG TERRACE

Pelter Bridge

steep slopes of BRANT BROWS

ROTHAY BRIDGE

AMBLESIDE 1¼ miles

0   100   200   300   400
Yards

Curious building by main road. Top floor is lived in, the ground floor is a garage.

Trees grow in abundance here, soaring up the steep hillsides to cascade over the river and road, threatening to engulf the houses in heavy foliage. The beech trees can make an autumn on their own. Bright and cheerful in sunshine, Rydal turns dark and depressive during wet weather. Wordsworth's gloomy character still haunts the hillsides.

Crossing the main road can be a terrifying experience as hoards of motorists charge to and from their favourite bits of Lakeland. Good job William isn't here to see it. He had enough of a scare when it was planned to bring the railway track through Rydal. Wordsworth was actively involved in the campaign against the railway, but to be on the safe side he bought shares in the railway company too.

Roadside cottages.

Church Cottage.

Wordsworth, never burdened by humility, decided that Rydal should have a church. As unofficial design consultant he picked a site handy for his own house. The resulting church of St Mary, finished in 1824, is a disappointment. One of the windows is dedicated to Dr Arnold, friend of the Wordsworth family. They, of course, had the best pew in the place – right in front of the pulpit.

Sheep now graze in the churchyard, but a much greater sacrilege has been done to the building itself; multi-coloured fairy lights hang from the gutterings. Dear, oh dear, what would William have thought. Was that the roar of passing traffic that I heard or was it someone turning in a grave at Grasmere?

St Mary's church.

Rydal Water and Loughrigg Fell.

Near the Glen Rothay Hotel a footbridge over the river leads to Rydal Water. A beautiful tranquil lake looked over by a single white house – Nab Cottage. This was once the home of Thomas De Quincey, writer and acquaintance of the Lake Poets' circle. He became the next tenant of Dove Cottage after the Wordsworths, who were most upset when De Quincey kept on the cottage as a store for his books after he moved to Rydal Water. Dated 1702, Nab Cottage is now a charming guest house.

Originally a 16th century cottage, Rydal Mount was owned by the Fleming family of Rydal Hall when the Wordsworth family took up residency in 1813. It is a surprisingly light and spacious house, the grandest they ever lived in. Now owned by a descendant of the poet and open to the public since 1970, the Mount contains a lot of his furniture, manuscripts and possessions.

Wordsworth landscaped the beautiful gardens and gave the field at the bottom to his daughter, Dora. Bright with hosts of golden daffodils in spring, it is still called Dora's Field.

Rydal Mount.

The very steep lane to Rydal Mount passes an amazing 17th century house almost hidden by exotic trees. Rydal Hall and park across the road was owned by the influential Fleming family for 400 years. Now the elegant hall belongs to a religious organisation and is not open to the general public.

Rydal Hall.

At Rydal Mount, Wordsworth lived the life of a grand old man of letters with gusto, as great people of the day trudged up the hill to pay him respect. Queen Victoria made him Poet Laureate and Lord Lowther elected him Distributor of Stamps for Westmorland, a kind of local tax collector – the only real job Wordsworth ever did.

He died at the age of 80 in 1850, a legend in his own lifetime and an even bigger one since.

Though Rydal is in no sense a village community, it is a lovely little spot with a tiny jewel of a lake to match.

Nab Cottage.

All Saints Church and Rose Cottage.

Satterthwaite

Cut off in a valley clearing of Grizedale Forest, this isn't a village you come across by chance.

I headed for it up the narrow road that runs north from Haverthwaite to Hawkshead. Pleasant, flat farmland all the way, punctuated by patches of trees with a surprising number of caravans and tents gathered round the many farms.

The road south from Hawkshead goes through continual forest. Not unattractive, though I found it a bit lonely.

Grizedale Forest is a huge, green carpet, more than twice the size of Lake Windermere and Coniston. Satterthwaite lies in a three mile long area of fields, enclosed on two sides by forested fells.

The 'thwaite' part of the village name is Old Norse for 'clearing', a legacy of the first settlers here. During the middle ages this area was part of Furness Abbey. Smoke from charcoal burners and iron smelters filled the valley. Well into the present century water driven mills produced bobbins and brushes from locally cut coppice wood.

Satterthwaite today is entirely residential, many villagers carrying on the traditional occupation of woodsmen with the Forestry Commission.

The Eagles Head.

130

I found parking in the village very frustrating, finally leaving my car half a mile outside and walking back.

To places like this with no shops or bus services, travelling shops are a vital life-line. The driver of one kept parking in my way as I tried to take photographs, making for some lively banter as we both made our way through the village. Cheerful ladies who came out to his shop were the only local people I saw on the quiet streets.

Central village.

The church porch and lychgate.

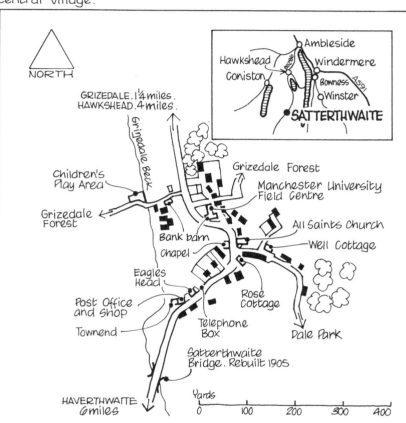

The centre of the village has a small walled green, some interesting cottages and the amazing All Saints Church, that looks like a carnival float parked up waiting for the procession to start. It's oddly built of dressed slate, with a too-short tower topped by fairy-tale castellations. The entrance porch, uniquely placed at an angle, has enough lead on the roof to keep Burglar Bill busy for a month.

Inside, the village children tell the story of the church in charming pictures hung round the walls. An old chapel used to stand here after being spared by Henry the Eighth at the dissolution of the Abbeys. It was replaced in 1840 by the present off-beat, yet very engaging building.

The village from the west

131

Across the road is the old schoolroom, built in 1848, now used as a small village hall.

Residents have done their best with the concrete council houses by the green, adding hedges and pretty gardens but they still look very crude. Surely it's not beyond councils to put up houses for rent that look reasonable?

Despite this niggle, I found Satterthwaite abounding in pretty houses, most of them with little wooden porches of different and imaginative designs. Fine examples of the art of the village woodworkers.

All Saints Church.

Townend and the Post Office.

Satterthwaite has two magnificent bank barns, built during the great days of farming. Neither of them is in agricultural use now. One is a store for equipment of the Manchester University Field Centre, the other is full of battery hens. Factory farming is not agriculture in my book.

The Post Office and gift shop is in an extension of a grand-looking white house on the edge of the village. Next door is the quaint, no-frills, Eagles Head public house, made out of two small cottages knocked into one. There are no other services in the village.

Well Cottage.

Manchester University Field Centre.

The lane to Breasty Haw.

In the large courtyard by the theatre building, brawny woodsmen were tossing chain saws into the backs of mud-spattered vans, ready for another assault on the green hordes.

I headed back down the sunlit valley where the trees were tinged with autumn colours, for a last look at Satterthwaite. It was beginning to feel like an old friend.

Outsiders with money to spend have discovered the village long before me. Barns were being converted, cottages done up, hanging baskets hung. I could see the attraction. Hassle, noise and aggression seem totally absent from this peaceful spot. I'm glad I found Satterthwaite. It had been a revelation.

A mile up the road is Grizedale, where once stood Grizedale Hall, a famous prisoner-of-war camp for German officers during the war. Since the hall was demolished in 1957, the ornamental grounds have been used as a caravan and camping site. Stone balustrades and steps remain, making the car park a rather grand affair.

Across the road, the feed store and stables of the Hall have been converted to the unusual 'Theatre in the Forest', where many cultural events are held, with appearances by top actors and musicians.

I'm not keen on forests, they make my imagination run riot. Too many scarey bed-time stories when I was young. Thousands of others like them though, flocking to enjoy the forest trails, visitor centre and picnic areas. The Forestry Commission try very hard to manage in a caring way. Although the uplands are planted with the much disliked spruce and fir trees, areas of larch have encouraged the growth of large deer herds. Work is also going on to re-establish the ancient oak forest – a thousand years after it was cleared by the Norsemen.

Grizedale Hall. (1905-1957.)

The Theatre in the Forest.

OLD MAN OF CONISTON. 2631'.

WETHERLAM 2502'.

CRINKLE CRAGS

PIKE O' BLISCO 2304'

BIRK FELL

BOWFELL 2960'

LANGDALE PIKES

From the road to Far Sawrey.

Near Sawrey

The area between Esthwaite Water and Windermere has some of the most luscious meadows in the whole of Lakeland. Carefully-placed patches of woods pattern the green fields like the park of a stately home. Most of this area is managed by the National Trust after it was left to them by Sawrey's most famous landowner and producer of children's books, Beatrix Potter.

The village is divided by half a mile into 'Near' and 'Far' sections. Probably referring to their distances from Hawkshead, the old administrative centre.

Coming from Hawkshead, the road passes Esthwaite Water, then from rising ground just before the village there's a sensational view over the lake and Hawkshead to a distant fell skyline of the Langdale Pikes and Wetherlam. Park by the children's playground on the edge of the village and walk back along the road for 200 yards. Don't miss this view.

A new way for me to Sawrey is along the west side of Windermere from Newby Bridge. Woodland most of the way with some pretty cottages and macho outdoor centres in the clearings. There's some pleasant views of the lake too, which looks like a broad river in these lower reaches. Near Sawrey has car parks but also many visitors, so you may have to cruise around a bit to find a space.

Many visitors to Near Sawrey seem to be earnest middle class parents giving their children a good dose of Beatrix Potter culture. This is reflected in the character of the village, made up of genteel cottages and serious guest houses decorously draped with large trees. A couple of picturesque farms have refined frontages, pretty gardens and woodpiles in the yards. I half expected to meet a duck wearing a mop cap.

The central village.

Garth Cottage.

There are no shops in Near Sawrey, though a tea-room serves tea on a lawn, edged by rose trees in a thoroughly English manner.

I like the east side of the village best, where the houses sit on the hillside looking over Esthwaite Water as if in an amphitheatre. Resplendent gardens spill down the slopes, tended by ruddy-cheeked country folk happy to pass the time of day.

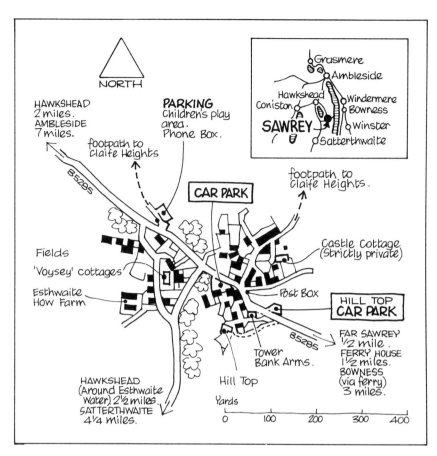

NORTH

HAWKSHEAD 2 miles. AMBLESIDE 7 miles.

B5285

footpath to Claife Heights

PARKING Children's play area. Phone Box.

CAR PARK

footpath to Claife Heights.

Fields

'Voysey' cottages

Esthwaite How Farm

Castle Cottage (strictly private)

Post Box

HILL TOP CAR PARK

B5285

FAR SAWREY ½ mile. FERRY HOUSE 1½ miles. BOWNESS (via ferry) 3 miles.

Tower Bank Arms.

Hill Top

HAWKSHEAD (Around Esthwaite Water) 2½ miles. SATTERTHWAITE 4¼ miles.

Yards

0   100   200   300   400

Grasmere
Ambleside
Hawkshead
Coniston   Windermere
SAWREY   Bowness
Winster
Satterthwaite

Voysey influenced design.

Among the maze of terraces and cottages there was plenty of curt notices advising nosey visitors to keep their distance. Fair enough – I wouldn't like strangers peering in my windows either. There is a tension here though. I felt like a schoolboy knowing I'd get teacher's ruler across my knuckles if I put a foot wrong.

Farmhouse by car park.

A terrace of cottages has a huge roof with dormer windows and four tall chimneys. This type of design spread into the countryside from the fine architect designed houses built around Windermere at the end of the 19th century. Though splendidly covered in roses, the building looked a bit dated to me.

I walked back to the centre of the village past the empty children's playground. All the kids were up the road buying Peter Rabbit badges.

Esthwaite How Farm & Esthwaite Water.

135

Beatrix Potter. (1865-1943)

Beatrix Potter was born in London to upper class parents who gave her a formal and restrictive upbringing. The family spent holidays in the Lake District where Beatrix found solace in wildlife and painting. She made little books for children that became very popular after she published the first one herself in 1900. Their success enabled Beatrix to buy Hill Top Farm as an artist's retreat.

After marrying local solicitor, William Heelis, she made a permanent home in the village at Castle Cottage, devoting the rest of her life to farms, Herdwick sheep and the countryside.

Beatrix Potter always wore clogs, looked like a favourite Granny, wasn't a bad farmer, but must have been a terrific businesswoman. She died at the age of 78 leaving 15 farms and 4000 acres of land to the National Trust.

Hill Top.

Castle Cottage.

Tower Bank Arms.

Hoards of people flock to Hill Top to see Beatrix Potter's furniture, her china and the delicate, original water colours for her books. Castle Cottage is only a field away. Quite pretty but tightly closed to all visitors.

A painting of the Tower Bank Arms can be seen in *The Tale of Jemima Puddle-Duck*. I was amazed to find the real thing looks almost the same, though Jemima had been replaced by Volvos.

Near Sawrey is a fairly ordinary village. Only Beatrix Potter makes it seem extra-ordinary.

Far Sawrey

Though only half a mile from its 'Near' neighbour, Far Sawrey is a different sort of a place altogether. Much less visited, so much less tense or determined to put on a good face. Pleasant though it is, this is the tradesman's entrance to the posh part of Sawrey just up the road. Here are the church, village hall and the small post office shop.

The main collection of buildings straggle up the west flank of Claife Heights, a tree-covered hill that stands beside Windermere. Parking is very difficult here. I squeezed onto some rough ground next to the telephone box.

Ignoring an inviting lane into the woods, I crossed the road to the Braithwaite Hall. It looks like a church but seems to be the village hall – a church hall, perhaps? Quite an attractive little building on an elevated position looking over the meadows and bits of woodland.

Down the hill, the Sawrey Hotel looked very striking with a large Union Jack fluttering from a pole in the garden. I was intrigued by this bit of flag-waving, the first I'd come across in these northern villages. Folks up here tend to be Cumbrians first and British second.

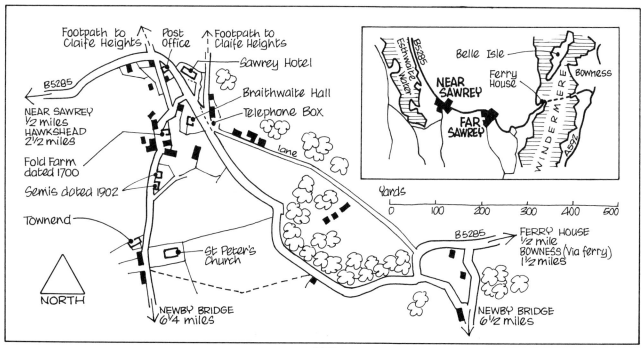

Braithwaite Hall.

St Peter's church is isolated in open fields. A handsome building with lancet windows and a tower. Erected in 1869, the church has some interesting stained glass, particularly the unusual window of the Good Samaritan. I took a seat beneath a broad larch tree in the churchyard to survey the wooded slopes of Claife Heights. Scene of an eerie, local ghost legend.

On dark and stormy nights 400 years ago, terrible cries for the Windermere ferry were heard coming across the lake from the Claife shore. Eventually, one brave ferryman rowed across the narrows to answer the pitiful calls. He returned next morning. Alone, speechless and horror-stricken. He died a few days later, never having spoken a word.

This was bad publicity for the ferry trade. Travellers were frightened away by the crier's continuing cries. Finally, the monks of Furness Abbey – ruthless businessmen themselves – laid the ghost in a desolate quarry on Claife Heights.

The Crier is commemorated by a bar in the Sawrey Hotel. Strangely, the modern ferry still doesn't put out on dark and stormy nights.

Fold Farm. Dated 1700.

There's an interesting variety of buildings down the road to the church. Fold Farm is an excellent example of a 17th century farm-house, with classic round chimneys and thick, rendered walls. Black and white sheepdogs yapped around the corners of slate-built barns in the yard.

It was a surprise to find some Victorian semis nearby, out on their own in the countryside. Though far more at home in a town, these brick-built, ornate houses still look impressive among the fields. Dated 1902, they are probably the most up-to-date buildings in the whole of the village, apart from a couple of modern bungalows I'd seen in Near Sawrey.

Sawrey Hotel.

Stately Windermere has attracted many rich outsiders. Royalty had large mansions built on the east shore. The railway was brought here to transport the upper classes into a gentle landscape that looked much like their own shire counties. Not for them the frightening fells, swirling with mist and mystery.

They would have found Sawrey much to their liking. As indeed, did I.

The Windermere ferry is a novel way to get to Far Sawrey. It takes walkers and 10 cars with their passengers across the narrow part of the lake near Bowness. The ferry is little more than a raft, pulling itself along on two chains strung under the water. Although crossings are about every ten minutes, it is normal to have to queue. Roadside signs tell motorists how long they may have to wait. The diesel-powered ferry is a great novelty and does save a lot of motoring miles.

Landing point on the Claife side of the lake is on a narrow-necked peninsula beside the headquarters of the Freshwater Biological Association. Here in the converted Ferry Hotel building, scientists study the water and marine life of all the Cumbrian lakes.

The surprisingly steep hill up from the lake towards Sawrey has some nice-looking cottages on the top. I paused by one to look across to the Bowness hillside of large, white villas, once the homes of Lancashire cotton barons. Yachts and power boats packed the lakeside in a grand show of affluence, untypical of Lakeland generally.

St. Peter's Church.

Townend.

Threlkeld

Having me as a resident during my teenage years doesn't seem to have caused lasting damage to Threlkeld. The village is far quieter these days, but it's due to being by-passed by the A66, rather than because I've left.

From either Penrith or Keswick, the three-lane highway is a racetrack all the way. There's some fabulous sights though. Especially of Blencathra at Scales, where the close-up views of airy mountain ridges are the best to be seen from any main road in the district.

The connoisseur's route to Threlkeld is from Thirlmere along St John's in the Vale. An exquisite little valley with a twinkling, tree-lined river winding beneath tremendous, rock-strewn cliffs. Centre stage is filled by the magnificent bulk of Blencathra.

Threlkeld village follows the twisting old road across the lower slopes of Gategill Fell. There is no public car park, though parking is easy with discretion.

An east wind often blows across Troutbeck Moor, making the village cold and bleak at times. Keswick folk describe Threlkeld as an 'extra coat' place.

Blease Road.

The village school.

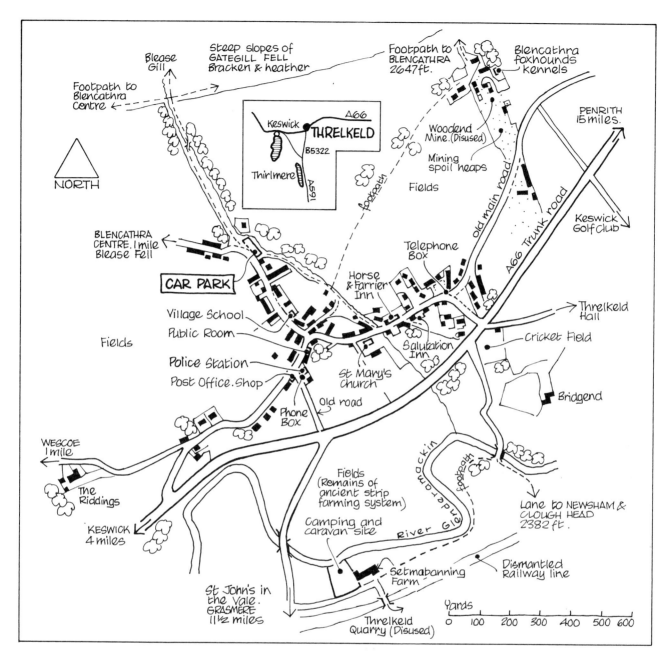

Steep slopes of GATEGILL FELL Bracken & heather

Blease Gill

Footpath to Blencathra Centre ←

Footpath to BLENCATHRA 2647ft.

Blencathra foxhounds kennels

PENRITH 15 miles.

Keswick A66 THRELKELD B5322 Thirlmere A591

NORTH

Woodend Mine.(Disused)

Mining spoil heaps

Fields

footpath

BLENCATHRA CENTRE. 1 mile Blease Fell ←

old main road

A66 Trunk road

Keswick Golf Club

Telephone Box

CAR PARK

Threlkeld Hall

Village School

Horse & Farrier Inn

Public Room

Cricket Field

Police Station

Salutation Inn

Fields

Post Office. Shop

St Mary's Church

Bridgend

Phone BOX

Old road

WESCOE 1 mile

Fields (Remains of ancient strip farming system)

Blenderhackin footpath

Lane to NEWSHAM & CLOUGH HEAD 2382 ft.

The Riddings

Dismantled Railway line

KESWICK 4 miles

Camping and caravan site

River Glenderamackin

St John's in the Vale. GRASMERE 11½ miles

Setmabanning Farm

Threlkeld Quarry (Disused)

Yards
0   100   200   300   400   500   600

Blencathra dominates the village. Jagged, soaring ridges rise almost from the cottage gardens, to meet at the pointed summit that is clearly seen from the streets below. The steep, monumentally-sculptured slopes are carpeted by heather and grass, frequently broken by shattered scree. Though often shrouded in mist for days on end, this is a much admired mountain.

South of the village, the Helvellyn range ends at the cliffs of Clough Head, towering over the more rounded slopes of Threlkeld Knotts.

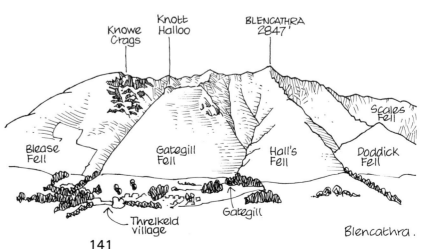

Knowe Crags

Knott Halloo

BLENCATHRA 2847'

Scales Fell

Blease Fell

Gategill Fell

Hall's Fell

Doddick Fell

Threlkeld village

Gategill

Blencathra.

Habitation of this valley began way back in the mists of pre-history. Castlerigg Stone Circle, near Threlkeld, is dated at 1400BC.

During the 10th century, Norse invaders joined with the Celts, who were living on Threlkeld Knotts, to establish a new settlement across the river. They called it 'Thrall's Spring' – Threlkeld. The river has kept its splendid Celtic name of Glenderamackin.

St Kentigern is said to have raised a cross here in 550AD, but it was to be another 1200 years before the present church was built.

Church Row.
The low building on the left is believed to be the oldest in the village.

St. Mary's Church.

Discovery of lead and zinc on Blencathra led to a spectacular – if short-lived – boom-time at Threlkeld. Around the turn of the century 100 men were employed at Gategill mine. To house them characteristic terraces of houses were built in the village, using slate waste from the workings.

The hills across the valley have been quarried for granite, that was used to build Thirlmere dam and as road surface chippings. Blasting stopped in 1980, but the scars still show. The old Penrith to Workington railway track that ran just below the quarry from 1864 to 1972 has now been turned into a scenic walk to Keswick. Fields around the village are still farmed, but with the decline of local industry Threlkeld has become completely residential.

St Mary's church was built in 1777. Stark and simple with a squat bell-tower left-over from an earlier thatched structure. Cut-off from the village by dark trees and a low position, the church has a sad and lonely air.

An old village custom is still carried on at weddings. During the service the churchyard gates are closed and tied by ropes. The happy couple are then held hostage until the bridegroom tosses handfuls of copper coins over the gates for village urchins to scramble for.

The Post Office & Shop.

Salutation Inn.

Threlkeld appears on the surface to be untouched by tourism – try buying a souvenir or even a cup of tea here! However, many cottages have become weekend retreats and canny locals rent out their own 'holiday lets'. An excellent 18 hole golf course has been developed on the outskirts of the village as a new attraction.

Visitors come to swarm all over Blencathra but villagers still walk it too. And graze sheep on the slopes, hunt foxes and run trail hounds. Not a lot has changed. Threlkeld remains the honest, rough and ready place that I remember with such affection.

Low House.

When I lived here there were four shops. Now only the post office remains. Close-by is the grand-looking Public Room, a place of many happy memories for me. A vast range of activities were held here. The usual Whist Drives and Harvest Suppers, but also West End farces performed by the local theatrical group, and wild Hunt Balls led by wailing accordion bands.

Nearby, Blease Road climbs past old cottages, across the fell to the Blencathra Centre. Once a TB isolation hospital with spectacular views, now converted to accommodation for lovers of outdoor pursuits.

Like most mining villages, Threlkeld once had many inns. Just two remain. The Horse and Farrier is one of the oldest in Cumbria. Over the door there is the inscription, CIG1688. The initials are those of Christopher and Grace Irton, then living at Threlkeld Hall. The Salutation Inn is of a much later date. Regular patrons here are of short stature, as the bar ceiling is exceedingly low.

Both pubs are blighted by monstrous inn signs, ugly enough to drive anybody to drink. A clever marketing ploy by the brewery, perhaps?

Horse and Farrier.

143

Road junction at centre of village and Brow Head, dated 1692.

Troutbeck

Easy to get to, emminently civilised and well-documented by historians and professors of vernacular architecture, Troutbeck is the darling of the media set. It is also achingly pretty and a devilishly difficult place to park a car.

The village is situated along the side of a long, green finger of valley that thrusts northwards from Windermere. Fortunately, the main road takes a lower route to Ullswater, leaving Troutbeck to bask in peace.

There's three narrow roads from the south that branch off the A591 to twist and climb their way here through pleasant countryside.

I like the road from the north over Kirkstone Pass. After the steady climb out of Patterdale, a stop on the top is a must. Here the wind is funnelled between high cliffs, often making standing straight-up a problem even before visiting the famous Kirkstone Pass Inn. At 1500 feet, this is one of the highest situated hostelries in Britain. The old coaching inn was built in 1840 by a long-time resident of Troutbeck, Parson Sewell.

Descent to the village is through bleak fell country where snow can linger long after Easter. There's some great elevated views over the valley, before the narrow road to Troutbeck is reached.

Spinning Gallery at High Green.

144

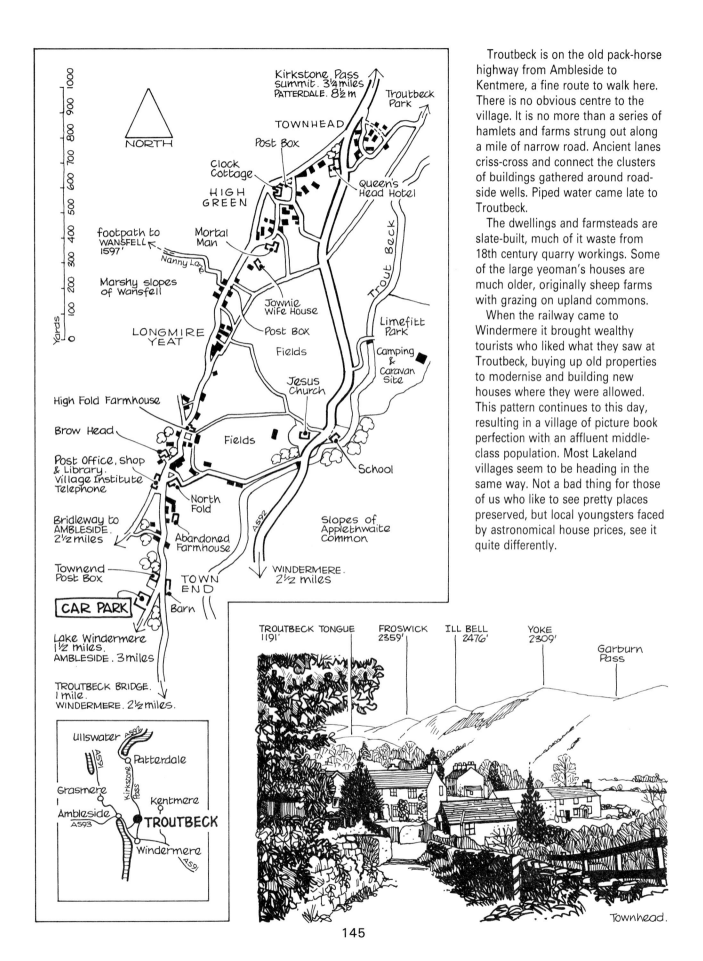

Map labels:

1000 900 800 700 600 500 400 300 200 100 0
Yards

NORTH

Kirkstone Pass
Summit. 3¾ miles
PATTERDALE. 8½ m

Troutbeck Park

TOWNHEAD

Post Box

Clock Cottage

Queen's Head Hotel

HIGH GREEN

footpath to WANSFELL 1597'

Mortal Man

Nanny Lane

Trout Beck

Marshy slopes of Wansfell

Jownie Wife House

Post Box

Limefitt Park

LONGMIRE YEAT

Fields

Camping & Caravan Site

Jesus Church

High Fold Farmhouse

Brow Head

Fields

Post Office, shop & Library. Village Institute Telephone

North Fold

School

A592

Bridleway to AMBLESIDE. 2½ miles

Abandoned Farmhouse

Slopes of Applethwaite Common

Townend Post Box

TOWN END

CAR PARK

Barn

WINDERMERE. 2½ miles

Lake Windermere 1½ miles. AMBLESIDE. 3 miles

TROUTBECK BRIDGE. 1 mile. WINDERMERE. 2½ miles.

Ullswater A592
A591
Patterdale
Grasmere
Kirkstone Pass
Kentmere
Ambleside A593
TROUTBECK
Windermere A591

TROUTBECK TONGUE 1191'   FROSWICK 2359'   ILL BELL 2476'   YOKE 2309'   Garburn Pass

Townhead.

Troutbeck is on the old pack-horse highway from Ambleside to Kentmere, a fine route to walk here. There is no obvious centre to the village. It is no more than a series of hamlets and farms strung out along a mile of narrow road. Ancient lanes criss-cross and connect the clusters of buildings gathered around road-side wells. Piped water came late to Troutbeck.

The dwellings and farmsteads are slate-built, much of it waste from 18th century quarry workings. Some of the large yeoman's houses are much older, originally sheep farms with grazing on upland commons.

When the railway came to Windermere it brought wealthy tourists who liked what they saw at Troutbeck, buying up old properties to modernise and building new houses where they were allowed. This pattern continues to this day, resulting in a village of picture book perfection with an affluent middle-class population. Most Lakeland villages seem to be heading in the same way. Not a bad thing for those of us who like to see pretty places preserved, but local youngsters faced by astronomical house prices, see it quite differently.

145

Clock Cottage.

High Green.

Troutbeck can only be appreciated on foot. I began at the north end, for me the best bit of this fascinating village.

The lanes around here are isolated by high, stone walls and can be very confusing. I was never sure where I was heading, though there was usually a nice surprise at the end. One was Clock Cottage, part of a group of old farm buildings added to and modernised in a most sympathetic manner. Farmers never bother with clocks much, so the one on the wall is quite unusual. It has stopped at a quarter to eleven. Time really does stand still here.

Nearby High Green is an amazing collection of fine houses and bank barns. A carefully-preserved spinning gallery is very picturesque. One house is dated 1686, a barn has a plaque of 1890.

The Mortal Man is a large, rambling building with splendid views around the valley. Originally the site of a 17th century inn, it was largely rebuilt when tourists began to flock here in the 19th century. I had a drink outside at one of the tables overlooking High Green. The bank barns were a grand sight, over-hung by dark trees and backed by the barren slopes of Applethwaite Common across the valley. This had been a lovely little area to explore.

Mortal Man.

Longmire Yeat.

Troutbeck's best-looking group of buildings is at Longmire Yeat. The house of that name is long and low with a stone in the chimney stack inscribed GB1649. A nearby gable end has a puzzling window immediately below a chimney stack. Behind the houses there's a glorious scene of slate and white-painted cottages, stone walls and colourful gardens, ancient lanes and distant mountains.

The Longmires are an old Troutbeck family. Margaret Longmire lived to the age of 104. She died in 1868 and is buried in the local churchyard. 'Yeat' is the Cumbrian dialect word for 'gate'.

The Queen's Head Inn is on the main road below High Green. Very much the Elizabethan coaching inn, with a gallery shaded by ancient oak trees. The restaurant has carved oak furniture, pride of place going to the regal 'Mayor's Chair'.

Most years since 1780 a 'Hunting Mayor' has been enthroned here. Duties are to see the Coniston Foxhounds off at the opening hunt, then to officiate at the jollifications in the inn at night. Recently, the holder of the office was the landlady of the Queen's Head. A rare chase for Woman's Lib into the male bastions of Cumbrian fox hunting.

Queen's Head Hotel.

'Jowie Wife House' is a curious name for a delightful white-fronted dwelling that appears to be split into two abodes. Stone-slabbed steps still lead to what used to be the first-floor granary, while a barn cut into the hillside has been converted to a garage. Hanging baskets and pink hydrangeas complete an idyllic picture. This is my favourite Troutbeck house.

Further on, near the post box, there's a large bank barn with an unusual hipped roof. Even more unusual – the barn has a chimney stack.

Jownie Wife House.

High Fold Farmhouse stands at the entrance to a small courtyard where 17th and 19th century houses compete with modern barn and granary conversions as holiday accommodation. Discreet notices in the windows were the only signs of commerciality I saw throughout the whole village. Lanes lead off to the north and south indicating the importance of this enclosure in earlier times.

Just beyond here the road narrows dramatically, to twist past another group of cottages topped by a great variety of interesting slate chimney stacks.

High Fold Farmhouse.

At the road junction next to Low Fold Farm, I contemplated the limited view from a wooden seat.

Suddenly, a flock of sheep swept up the hill round the corner. As if on a predetermined signal, a high gate into the farmyard opened. Then just before I was engulfed in wall-to-wall sheepskin rug, a dog ran ahead and turned the charging mob into the yard. The gate closed silently behind them.

Amazingly, I saw no human being at all!

Low Fold Farm.

Near the road junction there's Brow Head. Looking a bit tatty, but hardly surprising as it's nearly 300 years old. Yet another bank barn has 1868 inscribed over the door. Yeoman farmers of old certainly liked their barns big and solid-looking.

Similarly built is the Institute, the nearest thing Troutbeck has to a village centre. Entrance to the public hall on the top floor is from further up the hillside – bank barn principle again.

I found the ground floor a great surprise. Just inside the front door there's a remarkable reading room with glass-fronted bookcases around the walls. Curved-back chairs stand around a wooden table, almost filling the rest of the dusty room. Characters from Dickens would look quite at home sitting arguing here, with Mr Pickwick at their head.

An ordinary house door leads into the post office, as plain as a farmhouse kitchen. Stout-armed ladies in pinnies were dishing out cans of Coke to punk-haired youths in designer ski-jackets. It all looked very strange in these old-fashioned surroundings.

Outside the Institute a seat is strategically placed to take in a fine view across the valley.

The Institute.

Troutbeck refinement.

Abandoned farmhouse.

The derelict Elizabethan farmhouse is a rare building that escaped being 'improved' – but only by being abandoned in the 18th century before it could happen. Though a popular picture on glossy calendars I found it a sorry sight. Preservation orders have kept the desirable pile out of developer's hands. A shame in this case. Other old buildings in the village have been done-up with sensitivity, giving much pleasure to their owners and gawping visitors like me. Rather than be left to fall into a heap of rubble, this house could do the same.

Townend.

Of all historic houses in Troutbeck, the finest is undoubtedly Townend.

It was built in 1626 on the site of an earlier house, by George Browne, a wealthy yeoman wool-farmer whose family were well-established in the village. There is no electricity in the house, so the inside is authentically lit by daylight filtering through the small wood-mullioned windows.

Generations of Brownes all contributed to the magnificent carved panelling and wooden furniture in the house. A curious conglomeration of cupboards and drawers even incorporates a grand-father clock. Chairs used by the children and an elaborately-carved cradle are delightful. There's domestic utensils too, and a collection of oil lamps and pictures. Plus the Browne family papers.

This is not a hotch-potch of bits from many sources, they all belong in this house. A fascinating record of the life-style of one family through the ages.

Since 1947 the house has been owned by the National Trust who open it to the public on summer afternoons. It's not on their list of most visited properties, but none the worse for that. The delicate atmosphere of Townend would be ruined by coach loads of trippers tramping through.

I wandered back down the path through the garden, laid out from a 19th century photograph of Townend. Across the road there's a very fine 17th century bank barn with a spinning gallery. Here the Browne family stored wool fleeces until they were sold to merchants. The barn is not open to the public.

Townend bank barn.

150

The church is situated away from the village, beside the main road. It was built in 1736 on the site of an older structure, to serve all the valley. Troutbeck grew while other parts declined in population, leaving the church looking rather isolated today.

It has the unusual distinction of not having a patron saint, being simply called 'Jesus Church' instead. The plain building is beautifully proportioned with regular lancet windows. Castellations on the top of the tower are interestingly exactly the same as those on the tower of Grasmere church.

Inside, the massive beams are very impressive and probably came from the original 16th century building. The east window has colourful stained glass, designed in 1873 by Edward Burne-Jones, assisted by fellow 'Pre-Raphaelite' artists, Ford Maddox Brown and William Morris, while they were on holiday here.

Jesus church.

Across the road is the old village school, which together with the church and all of the village, was declared a conservation area in 1981 by the Lake District Special Planning Board.

I had a look at the river that gives the village its name. It was disappointingly overgrown. Not how I'd expected a trout beck to look.

One of the three lynch gates at the side of the churchyard led me into an old lane back to the village. The houses were all strung across the green hillside above me. What a pleasant place Troutbeck is. And likely to remain so. The villagers appear to have the financial clout to ensure it. Good.

The church and village school.

151

Underbarrow

I was confused here. The village is so scattered it was unclear where this one ended and the next began.

Underbarrow takes its name from Helsington Barrow, a 700 foot high limestone ridge that overlooks Kendal. But the ridge was over a mile away and not particularly noticeable from the village I was exploring. Was I in the right place? A chatty villager reassured me. He'd been all over the world and this was definitely Underbarrow. "Don't miss Tullythwaite House," he insisted after I'd told him what I was up to. "Where is it?" I enquired. His description of the route seemed to go on for miles, so I decided to impose my own village boundaries.

Underbarrow is at the cross roads of a network of minor roads going from Crook to Levens and Kendal to Crosthwaite. I arrived here from Crook where I had turned off the B5284 – a great road for escaping the traffic between Kendal and Bowness. This area is an interesting mix of farmland, rough common and outcrops of white limestone. The many farms and hamlets are connected by a maze of narrow roads and lanes. Though close to many tourist hot-spots, it is remarkably quiet and untouched by the outside world.

Thanking my world-traveller friend, I set off to explore the triangle of roads connecting the pub, church and High Gregg Hall.

High Gregg Hall.

152

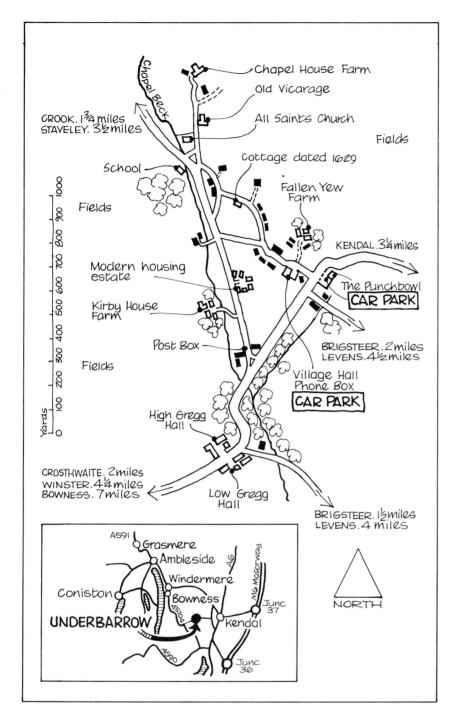

Chapel House Farm
Old Vicarage
All Saints Church

CROOK. 1¾ miles
STAVELEY. 3½ miles

Fields

Cottage dated 1629

School

Fields

Fallen Yew Farm

KENDAL. 3¾ miles

Modern housing estate

Kirby House Farm

The Punchbowl
CAR PARK

Post Box

BRIGSTEER. 2 miles
LEVENS. 4½ miles

Fields

Village Hall
Phone Box
CAR PARK

High Gregg Hall

CROSTHWAITE. 2 miles
WINSTER. 4¼ miles
BOWNESS. 7 miles

Low Gregg Hall

BRIGSTEER. 1½ miles
LEVENS. 4 miles

Yards
1000 900 800 700 600 500 400 300 200 100 0

A591 Grasmere
Ambleside
A6
Coniston
Windermere
Bowness
M6 Motorway
Junc 37
UNDERBARROW
Kendal
A5284
A591
A590
Junc 36

NORTH

The main huddle of buildings is on a breezy, low hill. I passed Fallen Yew Farm, looking quite old to me across a meadow bright with buttercups. The farm seems to have gone in for poultry houses and fence posts in a big way.

Though well cared for, the village hall is an ugly grey structure of corrugated tin sheeting. After this a row of cottages at the top of the hill was a welcome sight. One has a window that runs from almost ground level up to the eaves.

Round the corner was a row of neat modern bungalows. One had toys scattered all over the lawn and toddlers scattered all over the flower beds. I hadn't seen many children around the villages, most of them seem to be populated by people well past child rearing age. So it was good to see a younger family had moved in here.

Fallen Yew Farm.

I was now in a narrow lane edged by high grass verges and hedges. Wild flowers grew in abundance, demonstrating in a colourful way how depleted many of our roadsides have become. There were some lovely snow-white cottages along here, traditional Lakeland style with tiny windows and solidly-built stone porches.

A few more yards and I was back onto a proper road near All Saints Church. Dark and dramatic, the building looks a very extravagant design for a sparsely populated parish. Country churches don't usually need to draw attention to themselves so much.

However, it is an impressive cruciform building, with a tall porch turret topped by a short spire. Inside is unmemorable, though the parishioners are very proud of the old oil lamps that still hang from the roof. All Saints was built in 1869 on a site that has had a church for over 1000 years. The setting, beside Chapel Beck, is so perfect it must have been divinely provided for just this purpose.

The Punchbowl.

Cottage dated 1629

All Saints Church.

When horse-drawn coaches used to rattle round these roads, Underbarrow had three inns to serve the needs of man and beast. Now just the Punch Bowl carries on the tradition. Modern four-wheeled beasts cool off in the large car park.

Underbarrow pheasants are reputed to be very tasty. I saw none around the lanes. Nor any place serving them up on a plate. Apart from the pub, there is no place to eat, not even a shop.

A local cavalryman returned to live in the village after he had survived the Charge of the Light Brigade. He was luckier than the local pheasants.

Blissful by-way.

Trusting in my invaluable Ordnance Survey map, I expected to find a post office at the end of the road. Alas, it has gone. Underbarrow is totally shopless.

I did find Tullythwaite House though. Not too far away, up a very narrow road. It looked like an ordinary farm-house, but apparently this unlikely place had served-up fantastic food for many a year. Unfortunately the house was closed after just being sold, so I didn't get to see if pheasant was on the menu.

Chapel House Farm.

Down the lane by the church, the old vicarage has been converted into attractive smaller dwellings. Further along there's Chapel House Farm, a large impressive building on a hill with a lawn and attractive garden sloping away.

Most Underbarrow farm-houses are big and spacious, quite unlike their sturdy white-washed relatives in the wild fell regions. There is a great feeling of space to spare in this village. None of the older houses have to snuggle together to conserve valuable agricultural land.

I returned to the long straight stretch of the Crook road above Chapel Beck where lorries of a local transport company were parked among the trees. Lorry driving is a common occupation for the men of Cumbrian non-tourist villages.

Kirby House Farm is another grand-looking building. Some skeletal trees, victims of Dutch Elm Disease, spoiled the picture so out of respect for the dead, I've left them out of my drawing. Kirby House has a small orchard; as do other Underbarrow farms. It must be the limestone, many of the farms I know around Penrith have orchards too.

Kirby House Farm.

ILLGILL HEAD
1983ft

Wastwater
Screes

Wastwater

Slopes of
YEWBARROW
2058ft

Slopes of
KIRK FELL
2630ft.

Wasdale

Wasdale Head

Wasdale Head isn't a village. But with England's highest mountain, deepest lake, smallest church and biggest liar all to be found here, it's a niggardly detail.

One of the least accessible of Lakeland valleys, Wasdale still gets its share of visitors. In summertime the population of a temporary village of tents grows to many times that of the handful of permanent buildings.

Access to the valley by car is only from the West Cumbrian coastal plain, which means a long drive for anyone staying in the central Lake District. It could be quicker on foot. The five miles from Borrowdale over Styhead Pass is a very popular route here, so busy at times, it's like the M1 of mountain walks.

The motorist has a spectacular drive up Wasdale. First there's brooding, 258 feet deep Wast Water with its tremendous 2000 feet high backdrop of mountain scree. The broken rock faces, huge boulders and piles of shifting stones are awesome to behold.

Further along, the mighty Scafell range and the highest point in England come into sight across the water. The view of the fells up the lake is used as the emblem of the National Park.

Car parking in Wasdale is usually plentiful. That's on wet days. When the weather's fine, parking is difficult.

Coming here is like returning to the stone age. Stones are all over the place, washed down in ancient times from the surrounding stone-strewn fells. Farmers have collected them into great heaps in the fields. Those that haven't had all their sharp edges worn down have been built into high, substantial walls. The remarkable pattern of walled fields is very impressive when seen from the fellsides above.

Most visitors are drawn here by the magnificent mountains. Great lumps of volcanic rock, worn into pyramid shapes by the abrasive weather, often exposing jagged bands of exciting crags. This is well seen on Great Gable, the dalehead superstar that curiously seems to decrease in height as you get closer.

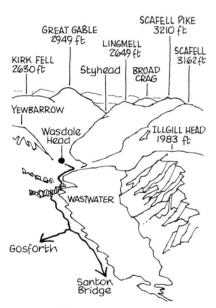

Wasdale from the south

British rock climbing virtually began on the crags of Wasdale Head. Wiry chaps from the towns in school plimsolls and ordinary suits scrambled up vertical rock towers with only bits of old towing rope for protection.

Nowadays the Wasdale car parks get littered by all manner of climbing aids, as hairy athletes in designer mountain clothes drape themselves with mysterious ironmongery and multicoloured ropes.

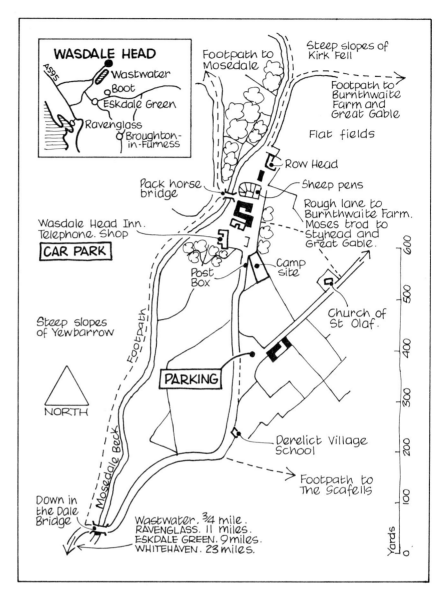

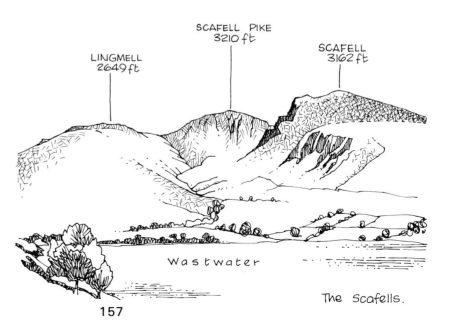

The Scafells.

During the 19th century the innkeeper at Wasdale Head was Will Ritson. His ability at telling the most amazing tall tales while keeping a straight face earned him the title of 'World's biggest liar'. A competition is held annually to find his present day successor. Any nominations?

The inn is a busy tourist centre these days, with accommodation, meals, bars, and a climbing shop in the yard. A pleasant river flows by, crossed by a picturesque pack-horse bridge. I walked along a grassy track onto the slopes of Kirk Fell. Quite steep, so I soon had a good view down the valley to the lake and Illgill Head. The few scattered buildings looked insignificant amongst such

Wasdale Head Inn.

grandeur. Between the barren fell slopes the trees and fields looked sharply green. Sunshine from a clear blue sky softened the shattered crags.

It was lovely, though landscape like this looks best in stormy weather. When shafts of sunlight and rolling banks of cloud combine with mountains and mist the result can be magical.

The relative smallness of St Olaf's Church is still an area of great controversy. Its rector, the Reverend Bowers, reckons it has the smallest cubic capacity of any used church in England. He should know, so I'll go along with his opinion.

The building is over 400 years old, built of rendered Wasdale stones and protected from the weather by 32 yew trees. Wooden roof beams

St. Olaf's Church.

The etching of Napes Needle on the south window.

I WILL LIFT UP MINE EYES UNTO THE HILLS FROM WHENCE COMETH MY STRENGTH

Interior of the church.

Great Gable from Wasdale Green.

I continued down the valley to pay my respects to the highest bit of rock in the country. When seen from here the proud stance of Scafell Pike is a bit overshadowed by the towering crags of Scafell. The range is probably best seen from Great Gable.

Wasdale is the most powerfully emotive of all Lakeland valleys. The harsh, oppressive mountains and the dark, silent lake can arouse deeply primitive passions. This is nature at its most base, there is no prettiness here.

I love it. For the scenery, the weather and the sombre brooding atmosphere.

inside are said to have come from wrecked Viking ships.

It's a delightful little place, though all the unpolished woodwork always reminds me of an old cattleshed.

Down the rough lane from the church is Wasdale Green, parking place for thousands of fell lovers and knee-deep in their worn-out bodies on a fine evening. It's a great place to get out the binoculars and scour the fearsome rock climbs on Great Gable from a safe distance. One of them, Napes Needle, is depicted in a tiny etching on one of the church windows.

Apart from all its other claims to fame, Wasdale is also home of the World's greatest fell runner, Joss Naylor. His speciality is to run up and down as many fells as he can in a given time. Like an astonishing 72 summits in 24 hours. You only have to look at the fells to see how difficult that is.

I took a more leisurely pace down the road to have a look at the old schoolroom. A sad sight now, boarded up and derelict. Surprising how small many of these village schools were. Strange too how 'improvements' in the education system has led to the closure of so many. Children from Wasdale now have to travel eight miles to school at Gosforth. Secondary school pupils often have to become boarders to complete their education.

The old school.

Pack horse bridge behind the inn.

159

Watendlath

No book of pretty-picture Lakeland is complete without Watendlath. The tiny tarn, pack-horse bridge and huddle of farm-houses has been photographed, filmed and painted in all manner of colourful compositions. Beautifully situated in a basin of gentle fells, it has a charm that is very difficult to resist. However, rushing straight to Watendlath is to miss one of the greatest pleasures of a visit – the way there.

Take the launch from Keswick up the lake to Ashness. Then walk up the fairly steep road to Ashness Bridge and Surprise View, both superlative view points. Through the wood, cross the river and follow the footpath along the bank to Watendlath. Four miles that can touch you for life.

Only slightly less spectacular is the shorter walk over the old pack-horse track from Rosthwaite. Thousands of boots have turned the Borrowdale side into something resembling a dried-up river bed, but the views make it all worthwhile. Looking down on Watendlath from the path is another photographer's favourite.

Steps End Farm.

160

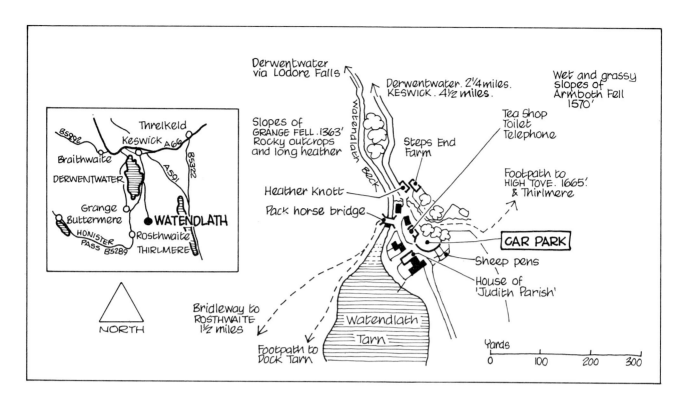

Derwentwater via Lodore Falls

Derwentwater. 2¼ miles. KESWICK. 4½ miles.

Wet and grassy slopes of Armboth Fell 1570'

Slopes of GRANGE FELL .1363' Rocky outcrops and long heather

Tea Shop Toilet Telephone

Steps End Farm

Footpath to HIGH TOVE. 1665' & Thirlmere

Heather Knott

Pack horse bridge

CAR PARK

Sheep pens

House of 'Judith Parish'

NORTH

Bridleway to ROSTHWAITE 1½ miles

Footpath to Dock Tarn

Watendlath Tarn

Yards
0   100   200   300

Inset map: B5292 Threlkeld Keswick A66 Braithwaite DERWENTWATER A591 B5322 Grange Buttermere WATENDLATH HONISTER PASS B5289 Rosthwaite THIRLMERE

This is a classic example of a Lake District 'hanging valley'. As melting glacial ice fashioned the large valleys, it also left little sub-troughs at higher levels, Watendlath Beck drops nearly 600 feet before joining Derwentwater. The final descent is very quick – over Lodore Falls.

Furness Abbey records mention Watendlath as part of their estate in 1209. An ancient field system can still be seen at the south end of the tarn. Now the farms are owned by the National Trust who ensure that traditional sheep farming is still carried on.

First settlement of Watendlath goes back to the Norsemen of the 10th century, who named the valley 'Vatns Endi', meaning 'end of the lake'. Nowadays the invaders carry cameras rather than double-headed axes.

From slopes of Armboth Fell.

From slopes of Grange Fell.

Inset: WATENDLATH — Grange Fell — Ladore Falls — GRANGE. The 'hanging' valley of Watendlath. DERWENTWATER

161

House of 'Judith Paris'.

Judith Paris is a fictitious character from the famous *Herries Chronicle* books written by Hugh Walpole. She lived at Watendlath with her husband, George Paris, who used the valley as a hideout from his smuggling activities at Whitehaven.

In 1937, Walpole had to settle a dispute between two Watendlath residents. Both claimed to live in the 'Judith Paris' house. A diplomat of the old school, Walpole declared that he had not based the house of his heroine on any one building in the hamlet.

Despite this, a farm-house carries a slate sign today that says it is 'The home of Judith Paris'.

The tiny hamlet is a disorganised collection of slate-built farms, barns and outbuildings. Some are rendered and painted white in the modern Lakeland fashion. Drystone walls and some lovely trees add the rural romantic charm. A tall Scots Pine tree has been a prominent feature of Watendlath for years.

What looks like a converted barn at Steps End Farm has recently had its inappropriate steel-framed windows replaced by some far more in keeping with the surroundings.

The approach from Borrowdale.

The pack horse bridge.

Watendlath used to be a resting place on a main pack-horse track that ran east to west across the valleys.

The pack horse bridge is constantly recorded for posterity around the world by multitudes of clicking cameras. It does make a splendid picture with ducks – and often children – splashing in the river.

Watendlath has very little in the way of amenities these days. There's only the old farm-house that sells teas during the summer.

A corner of the car park.

The last time I was at Watendlath a National Trust Land Rover had set-up shop, selling trinkets and itself to the public.

I'm full of admiration for this worthy organisation. Being asked to give a few coins after enjoying the fantastic freedom of the fells is one of the best value-for-money deals ever.

The Trust is not a Government-run body – thank goodness. It is an independent charity that relies on contributions from people like you and me for its funding.

Leading light of the foundation of the Trust was Canon Rawnsley of Crosthwaite Church, Keswick. Their first acquisition in the Lake District was Brandelhow Wood on the shores of Derwentwater, in 1902. The Trust is now the largest landowner in the Lakes, with over 90,000 acres, plus the care of another 14,000. It owns lakes, mountains, farms, cottages, pubs, famous houses, and sheep. Without them the Lake District would not be the much-admired place it is today.

Despite this, the National Trust still has its critics. My own gripe is the military style of its shop staff. Khaki uniforms, peaked hats and shining black boots can be a bit off-putting when you're buying a little bag of lavender for a loved one. They're all fine chaps, I'm sure, but I prefer local accents to the clipped delivery of the officer classes. The National Park rangers seem far more approachable.

But this is nit-picking – not literally, Sir! – places like Watendlath are a great tribute to the Trust's conservation efforts. Rather than becoming a Lakeland set-piece, this is still a place where people live and work. Lines of washing seem to perpetually billow in the wind. Sheep droppings speckle the lanes. Though always blissfully beautiful, Watendlath is also ALIVE.

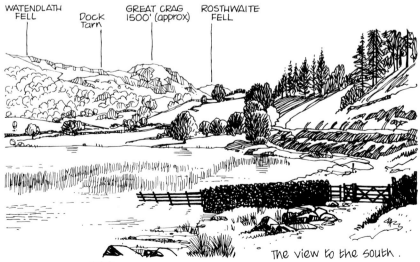

WATENDLATH FELL

Dock Tarn

GREAT CRAG 1500' (approx)

ROSTHWAITE FELL

The view to the south.

Winster

Compston House. (on the right.)

It took me a couple of visits before I discovered the delights of Winster. The extent of this scattered community was something I missed first time around.

On leaving busy Bowness, the main A5014 road goes straight into peaceful countryside, then climbs a couple of miles to Winster.

Coming north from Levens, the road goes through the pretty Lyth Valley beneath Whitbarrow, a great lump of limestone that dominates the area.

Winster is situated in a wide, shallow valley of green fields, stone walls, and patches of woodland. A pleasant, peaceful, but undramatic landscape. Compact farmsteads form the backbone of the village, though there's usually a good walk between them.

I almost missed the handful of roadside houses so had to double back along the road to find somewhere to park. A piece of rough ground next to a phone box was the only place.

Across the road there was a closed-down schoolroom, a familiar sight these days. This one is used as a village hall, so it has found some useful work to do after its education has finished.

I headed north along the main road that was edged by a wonderful display of wild flowers and shrubs. They were quite remarkable and seem to be a feature of this area.

Compston House and its neighbour are picturesque, 17th century Lakeland cottages. Colourful tumbling gardens make them a much-admired sight.

Further on, near the cross-roads that mark the edge of the village, there's High Mill, a greatly extended old farm sheltered by trees atop of a rocky knoll. An extensive view across the valley from here promised pleasures to come.

High Mill.

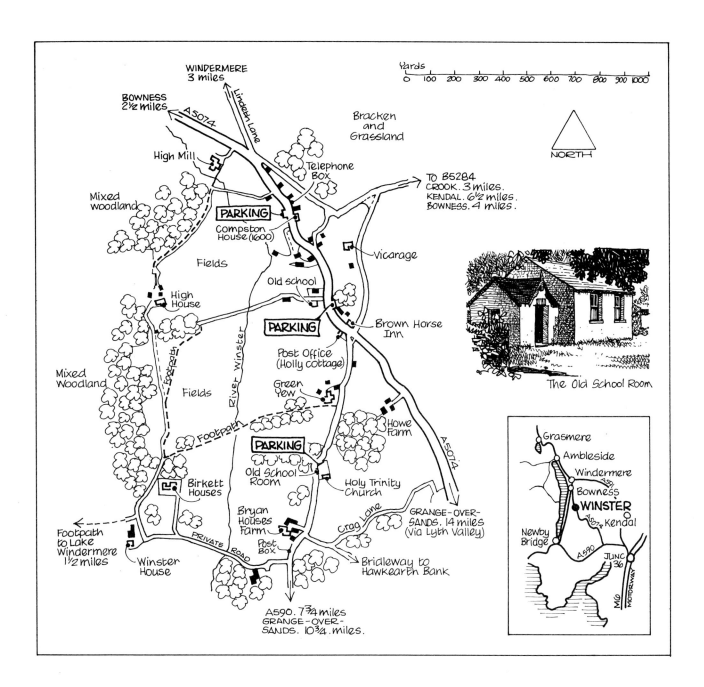

WINDERMERE
3 miles

BOWNESS
2½ miles

A5074

Lindeth Lane

High Mill

Mixed woodland

Telephone Box

Bracken and Grassland

Yards
0 100 200 300 400 500 600 700 800 900 1000

NORTH

PARKING

Compston House (1600)

TO B5284
CROOK. 3 miles.
KENDAL. 6½ miles.
BOWNESS. 4 miles.

Fields

Vicarage

Old school

High House

PARKING

Brown Horse Inn

River Winster

Post Office
(Holly cottage)

Mixed Woodland

Footpath

Fields

Green Yew

The Old School Room

Howe Farm

Footpath

PARKING

Old School Room

Holy Trinity Church

A5074

Grasmere
Ambleside
Windermere
Bowness
WINSTER
Kendal
Newby Bridge
JUNC 36
M6 MOTORWAY
A590

Birkett Houses

Bryan Houses Farm

Post Box

Crag Lane

GRANGE-OVER-
SANDS. 14 miles
(via Lyth Valley)

Footpath
to Lake
Windermere
1½ miles

Winster House

PRIVATE ROAD

Bridleway to
Hawkearth Bank

A590. 7¾ miles
GRANGE-OVER-
SANDS. 10¾ miles.

The Old School Room

The Winster valley from near Winster House.

As I eventually discovered, Winster is not just a village, it is a whole valley. A broad expanse of rolling fields broken by hillocks and outcrops of limestone, many crowned by attractive tufts of trees. Denser woodland grows on the hills to the west and south.

Winster should be judged on the area rather than first impressions of the few buildings along the main road. On that basis it is a splendid place to wander and relax in peace.

I sauntered back south from High Mill along a narrow lane. It was dark and gloomy. A condition that was affecting me too. Even a group of excellent barn conversions by the main road failed to lift my spirits.

Further along, the little post office is appealingly housed in Holly Cottage. But as I have a young daughter called Holly it only reminded me of my family 200 miles away. Yes, the intrepid explorer of darkest Lakeland was homesick!

Food, drink and company can sometimes give solace, so the pub across the road seemed to be the answer.

Holy Trinity Church.

The Post Office.

The plain Church of the Holy Trinity stands alone in wooded surroundings. It was built in 1875 from stone quarried from an outcrop just across the road. Inside there's some curious texts on wooden tablets and an impressive east window.

A churchyard war memorial is starkly beautiful near an ancient schoolroom, almost lost beneath hanging trees.

The War Memorial.

The Brown Horse Inn is not one of the Lake District's great beauty spots. A hotch-potch of wooden tables, slate tiles, signs and faded bunting make it as picturesque as Morecambe sea front. Still it was a pub and in my mood that was enough.

Inside, it was all very different. Comfortable and friendly. Scampi and chips with a glass of the brown nectar went down a treat. I returned to the streets refreshed and heartened, to head down the lane to the church.

Brown Horse Inn.

Birkett Houses is an astonishing sight. A sprawling, medieval manor house, with stone-mullioned windows and an extensive ornamental garden. The grey, sombre building has sprouted many chimneys. Some are in sections that decrease in diameter as they get higher, like huge telescopes stood on end.

It looks the kind of house that used to have the hounds set on nosey-parkers, so I didn't venture too close. Birkett Houses is now a very atmospheric country hotel.

Bryan Houses Farm.

Further along the road there's Bryan Houses Farm. It looks quite ancient with a picturesque yard and two fine bank barns. This used to be the home of Jonas Barber, a well-known maker of grandfather clocks, 300 years ago. A later resident was William Pearson, a poet and naturalist who showed fellow wordsmith Wordsworth around the valley. He was apparently well-pleased with his tour.

I didn't have the benefit of a poetic companion, but I was beginning to discover the appeal of this area.

A private road leads across the valley, so ensuring that my boots were clean, I set off down the hill. Beyond some attractive woodland the road crosses the discrete River Winster.

Winster House.

Birkett Houses.

Winster House is a fine-looking Georgian house with a huge barn, very prominent in the Winster landscape on the edge of a wood. A track heads north from here, passing more farms to complete a round tour of the valley near High Mill.

This village is never going to tempt loads of tourists away from the commercialised amusements of Bowness. However, to those eager for simpler pleasures, Winster could be a memorable day out. The three mile walk around the valley seems the best way to get full benefit. Carefully timed, of course, to include scampi and chips at the Brown Horse Inn.

WALK I ROSTHWAITE - GRANGE - WATENDLATH. 9 miles

Jagged volcanic crags, sparkling rivers, verdant woods, a premier lake, a tranquil tarn and superb mountain scenery combine to make this area one of the most popular in the Lake District. The profusion of humanity can be quite horrendous! But, given a clear, sunny, autumn day there is no other place I'd rather be.

Start this route at any point and split it up into manageable lengths if you wish. I prefer to go in a clockwise direction. There is some uphill work but a fit adult should have no problems.

Don't leave your start until the afternoon. Borrowdale is very invigorating in the morning!

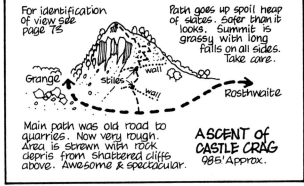

For identification of view see page 73

Path goes up spoil heap of slates. Safer than it looks. Summit is grassy with long falls on all sides. Take care.

Main path was old road to quarries. Now very rough. Area is strewn with rock debris from shattered cliffs above. Awesome & spectacular.

ASCENT of CASTLE CRAG 985' Approx.

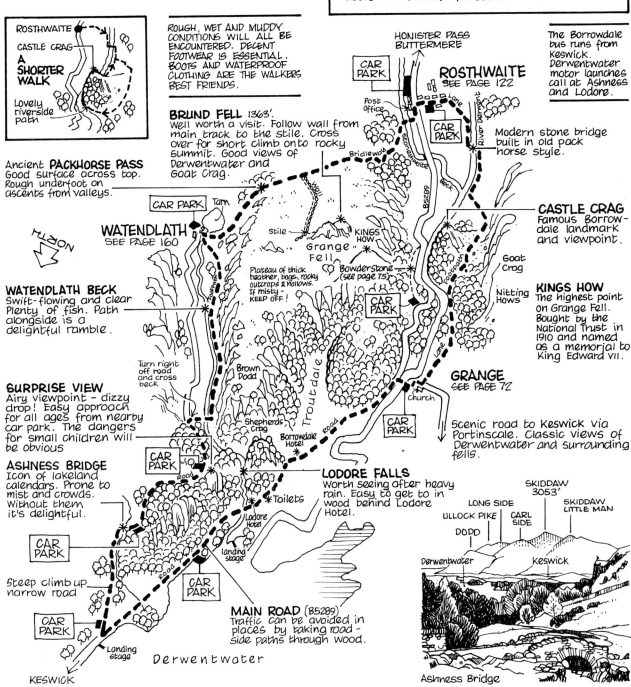

A SHORTER WALK
Lovely riverside path

ROUGH, WET AND MUDDY CONDITIONS WILL ALL BE ENCOUNTERED. DECENT FOOTWEAR IS ESSENTIAL. BOOTS AND WATERPROOF CLOTHING ARE THE WALKERS BEST FRIENDS.

BRUND FELL 1363'.
Well worth a visit. Follow wall from main track to the stile. Cross over for short climb onto rocky summit. Good views of Derwentwater and Goat Crag.

The Borrowdale bus runs from Keswick. Derwentwater motor launches call at Ashness and Lodore.

Modern stone bridge built in old pack horse style.

Ancient **PACKHORSE PASS**
Good surface across top. Rough underfoot on ascents from valleys.

CASTLE CRAG
Famous Borrowdale landmark and viewpoint.

KINGS HOW
The highest point on Grange Fell. Bought by the National Trust in 1910 and named as a memorial to King Edward VII.

WATENDLATH BECK
Swift-flowing and clear. Plenty of fish. Path alongside is a delightful ramble.

Plateau of thick heather, bogs, rocky outcrops & hollows. If misty - KEEP OFF!

GRANGE SEE PAGE 72

Scenic road to Keswick via Portinscale. Classic views of Derwentwater and surrounding fells.

SURPRISE VIEW
Airy viewpoint - dizzy drop! Easy approach for all ages from nearby car park. The dangers for small children will be obvious

ASHNESS BRIDGE
Icon of lakeland calendars. Prone to mist and crowds. Without them it's delightful.

Steep climb up narrow road

MAIN ROAD (B5289)
Traffic can be avoided in places by taking road-side paths through wood.

LODORE FALLS
Worth seeing after heavy rain. Easy to get to in wood behind Lodore Hotel.

WATENDLATH SEE PAGE 160

ROSTHWAITE SEE PAGE 122

SKIDDAW 3053'
LONG SIDE
ULLOCK PIKE
CARL SIDE
SKIDDAW LITTLE MAN
DODD
Derwentwater
Keswick

Ashness Bridge

WALK 2 GLENRIDDING - PATTERDALE - HARTSOP. 8 miles.

This is a tour of contrasts. There's a proud and picturesque lake, another plain and unpraised. Some close-cropped meadows and primeval mountain ranges. Lonely dales and busy roads. Barren rock screes and soft woodland. Tourist tat and traditional gentility.

Most of the route is along roads and lanes around the flat valley floor. Done as a single walk it can be very satisfying.

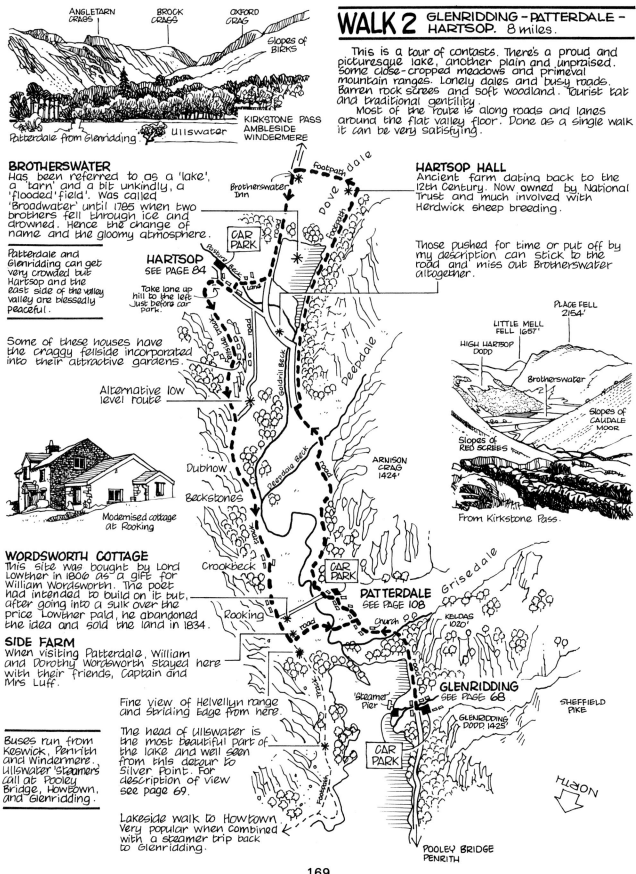

Patterdale from Glenridding.

ANGLETARN CRAGS — BROCK CRAGS — OXFORD CRAG — Slopes of BIRKS — Ullswater — KIRKSTONE PASS AMBLESIDE WINDERMERE

BROTHERSWATER
Has been referred to as a 'lake', a 'tarn' and a bit unkindly, a 'flooded' field'. Was called 'Broadwater' until 1785 when two brothers fell through ice and drowned. Hence the change of name and the gloomy atmosphere.

Patterdale and Glenridding can get very crowded but Hartsop and the east side of the valley valley are blessedly peaceful.

Some of these houses have the craggy fellside incorporated into their attractive gardens.

Alternative low level route

Modernised cottage at Rooking

HARTSOP
SEE PAGE 84

Take lane up hill to the left. Just before car park.

WORDSWORTH COTTAGE
This site was bought by Lord Lowther in 1806 as a gift for William Wordsworth. The poet had intended to build on it but, after going into a sulk over the price Lowther paid, he abandoned the idea and sold the land in 1834.

SIDE FARM
When visiting Patterdale, William and Dorothy Wordsworth stayed here with their friends, Captain and Mrs Luff.

Buses run from Keswick, Penrith and Windermere. Ullswater 'steamers' call at Pooley Bridge, Howtown, and Glenridding.

Fine view of Helvellyn range and Striding Edge from here.

The head of Ullswater is the most beautiful part of the lake and well seen from this detour to Silver Point. For description of view see page 69.

Lakeside walk to Howtown. Very popular when combined with a steamer trip back to Glenridding.

HARTSOP HALL
Ancient farm dating back to the 12th Century. Now owned by National Trust and much involved with Herdwick sheep breeding.

Those pushed for time or put off by my description can stick to the road and miss out Brotherswater altogether.

From Kirkstone Pass.

PLACE FELL 2154' — LITTLE MELL FELL 1657' — HIGH HARTSOP DODD — Brotherswater — Slopes of CAUDALE MOOR — Slopes of RED SCREES

Brotherswater Inn — CAR PARK — footpath — Dovedale — Deepdale — Goldrill Beck — Deepdale Beck — ARNISON CRAG 1424' — CAR PARK — PATTERDALE SEE PAGE 108 — Grisedale — Church — KELDAS 1020' — Dubhow — Beckstones — Crookbeck — Rooking — road — 'Steamer' Pier — Track — CAR PARK — Footpath — GLENRIDDING SEE PAGE 68 — GLENRIDDING DODD 1425' — SHEFFIELD PIKE — NORTH — POOLEY BRIDGE PENRITH

169

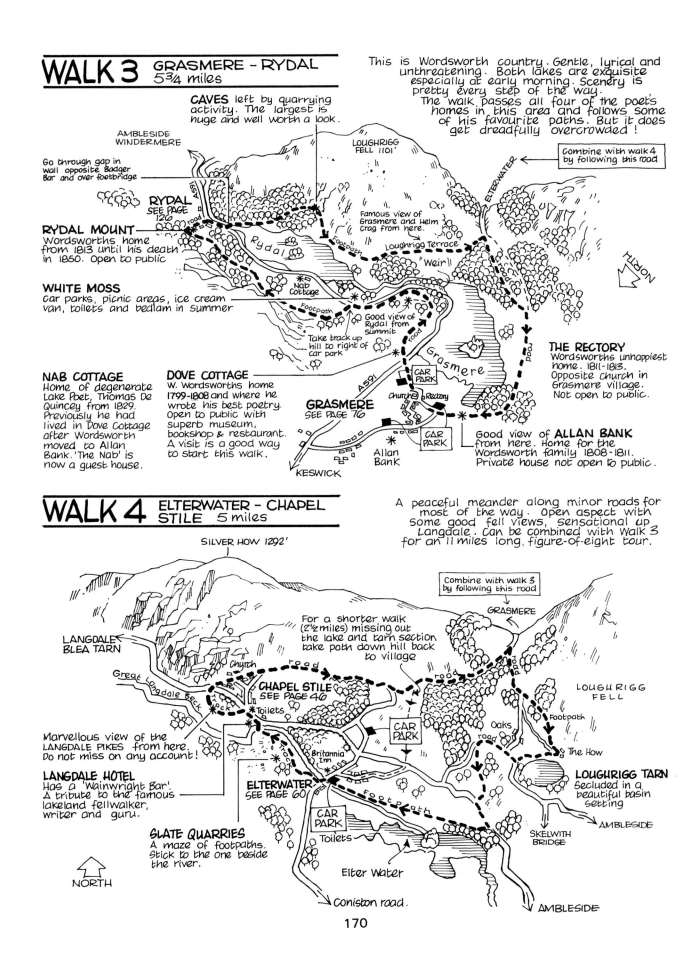

WALK 3 GRASMERE - RYDAL 5¾ miles

This is Wordsworth country. Gentle, lyrical and unthreatening. Both lakes are exquisite especially at early morning. Scenery is pretty every step of the way.
The walk passes all four of the poet's homes in this area and follows some of his favourite paths. But it does get dreadfully overcrowded!

Combine with walk 4 by following this road

AMBLESIDE WINDERMERE

LOUGHRIGG FELL 1101'

ELTERWATER

Go through gap in wall opposite Badger Bar and over footbridge

NORTH

CAVES left by quarrying activity. The largest is huge and well worth a look.

RYDAL SEE PAGE 126

RYDAL MOUNT — Wordsworths home from 1813 until his death in 1850. Open to public

Famous view of Grasmere and Helm Crag from here.

Loughrigg Terrace

Rydal

"Weir"

Nab Cottage

WHITE MOSS Car parks, picnic areas, ice cream van, toilets and bedlam in summer

Footpath

Good view of Rydal from summit

Take track up hill to right of car park

Grasmere

NAB COTTAGE Home of degenerate Lake Poet, Thomas De Quincey from 1829. Previously he had lived in Dove Cottage after Wordsworth moved to Allan Bank. 'The Nab' is now a guest house.

DOVE COTTAGE — W. Wordsworths home 1799-1808 and where he wrote his best poetry. Open to public with superb museum, bookshop & restaurant. A visit is a good way to start this walk.

CAR PARK

Church Rectory

GRASMERE SEE PAGE 76

A591

CAR PARK

Allan Bank

KESWICK

THE RECTORY Wordsworths unhappiest home. 1811-1813. Opposite Church in Grasmere village. Not open to public.

Good view of **ALLAN BANK** from here. Home for the Wordsworth family 1808-1811. Private house not open to public.

WALK 4 ELTERWATER - CHAPEL STILE 5 miles

A peaceful meander along minor roads for most of the way. Open aspect with some good fell views, sensational up Langdale. Can be combined with Walk 3 for an 11 miles long, figure-of-eight tour.

SILVER HOW 1292'

Combine with walk 3 by following this road

GRASMERE

For a shorter walk (2½ miles) missing out the lake and tarn section take path down hill back to village

LOUGHRIGG FELL

LANGDALE BLEA TARN

Great Langdale Beck

Church

CHAPEL STILE SEE PAGE 46

Toilets

road

road

Footpath

The How

road

Oaks

CAR PARK

Marvellous view of the LANGDALE PIKES from here. Do not miss on any account!

Britannia Inn

LOUGHRIGG TARN Secluded in a beautiful basin setting

LANGDALE HOTEL Has a 'Wainwright Bar'. A tribute to the famous lakeland fellwalker, writer and guru.

ELTERWATER SEE PAGE 60

Footpath

CAR PARK

Toilets

AMBLESIDE

SKELWITH BRIDGE

NORTH

SLATE QUARRIES A maze of footpaths. Stick to the one beside the river.

Elter Water

Coniston road.

AMBLESIDE

170

Lorton.

Bibliography

These are my favourite Lakeland reading. Books that in one way or another have helped me produce my own.

A. Wainwright. *Pictorial Guide to the Lakeland Fells.* Seven volumes. Westmorland Gazette. 1955-63.
The Old Master's astonishing works of art and research. Bound into one big book these are what I'd take with me to the Desert Island.

Hunter Davies. *A Walk Around the Lakes.* Hamlyn. 1979.
Still the best Lake District read there is. Hunter at his very best.

Hunter Davies. *The Good Guide to the Lakes.* Forster Davies. 1984.
Packed with good solid information, though the Davies schoolboy enthusiasm gets a bit wearing at times.

Norman Nicholson. *The Lakes.* Robert Hale. 1977.
Another splendid read with plenty of detail, delivered in Nicholson's fluent, poetic prose.

Millward and Robinson. *The Lake District.* Eyre Methuen. 1974.
A huge historic and geological study. Not half as dry as it sounds.

R. W. Brunskill. *Vernacular Architecture of the Lake Counties.* 1974.
A scholarly tome with good illustrations.

Trevor Haywood. *Walking with a camera in Herries Lakeland.* Fountain Press. 1986.
Stretches the Herries association at times, but has plenty of atmospheric photographs.

Printed in Great Britain by Martin's of Berwick